THE BIRDS

. . . .

Camille Paglia

 Publishing

First published in 1998 by the
BRITISH FILM INSTITUTE
21 Stephen Street, London W1P 2LN

The British Film Institute
is the UK national agency with
responsibility for encouraging the arts
of film and television and
conserving them in the national interest.

British Library Cataloguing-in-Publication Data
A catalogue record for this book is available from the British Library

ISBN 0–85170–651–7

Series design by
Andrew Barron & Collis Clements Associates

Typesetting by
D R Bungay Associates, Burghfield, Berks.

Printed in Great Britain by Norwich Colour Print

CONTENTS

. . . .

Melanie Daniels (Tippi Hedren) on the wharf at Bodega Bay

'THE BIRDS'
....

In his technically most difficult film, *The Birds* (1963), Alfred Hitchcock directly addresses the theme of destructive, rapacious nature that was always implicit in his fascination with crime. Federico Fellini called the film an 'apocalyptic poem'.[1] I place *The Birds* in the main line of British Romanticism, descending from the raw nature-tableaux and sinister femmes fatales of Coleridge. Overwhelmed by the film when I first saw it as an impressionable teenager, I view it as a perverse ode to woman's sexual glamour, which Hitchcock shows in all its seductive phases, from brittle artifice to melting vulnerability.

Because of his suspense-anthology television show, *Alfred Hitchcock Presents*, which premiered in 1955 and ran for a decade, Hitchcock existed as a powerful personality apart from his films for my post-war generation in the United States. His lugubrious, British formality, mordant irony (daringly directed against the show's commercial sponsors), and ghoulish, self-satirising pranks were an oasis of originality amid the general banality of a culture whose ideal types were Doris Day and Debbie Reynolds. That *Psycho* (1960), which stunned and terrified us, mirrored the real-life Hitchcock's macabre genius was easy for us to imagine, since we felt we already knew him.

Aside from a grainy screening of *North by Northwest* (1959) at a school function, *Psycho* was my sole experience of Hitchcock the film director before I saw his subsequent release, *The Birds*, which premiered three years later. Reviews were sharply unkind to its leading lady, Tippi Hedren, a Hitchcock discovery who was making her debut. In retrospect, I see that older viewers were used to a galaxy of established Hitchcock stars like Ingrid Bergman and Grace Kelly, whose sensibility belonged to a slightly earlier era. Because of *The Birds* and its spellbinding successor, *Marnie* (1964), both of which I saw in brilliant colour in widescreen commercial theatres, Tippi Hedren was and remains for me the ultimate Hitchcock heroine.

As I watched *The Birds* again and again on late-night television over the decades, certain key themes emerged for me: captivity and domestication. In this film, as in so many others, Hitchcock finds woman captivating but dangerous. She allures by nature, but she is chief artificer in civilisation, a magic fabricator of persona whose very smile is an arc of deception. With profound feeling for architecture, Hitchcock sees the house in historical terms as both safe haven and female trap. Ten thousand years ago, when man the nomad took root in one place, he brought animals with him into human service. But domestication was to be his fate too, as he fell under architecturally reinforced female control. *The Birds* charts a return of the repressed, a release of primitive forces of sex and appetite that have been subdued but never fully tamed. Because of Hitchcock's personal engagement with these unsettling themes, the film is worked out in almost fanatical detail, to a degree perhaps unparalleled in his oeuvre. The more microscopically this film is studied, the more it reveals.

The original idea for *The Birds* came from Daphne du Maurier's 1952 story of the same name, which had been reprinted in an *Alfred Hitchcock Presents* anthology. Hitchcock had already based two screenplays on du Maurier novels: *Jamaica Inn* became a rather stodgy 1939 pirate film that confirmed Hitchcock's self-confessed lack of 'feeling' for period pieces, but he turned *Rebecca* into a haunting masterpiece, the 1940 melodrama that began his Hollywood period.[2] Du Maurier's 'The Birds' takes place on the same cold, wind-swept, rocky Cornish coast as *Jamaica Inn*. Though there is no Gothic manor house, the story's bleak atmosphere and ferocious weather resemble those of the great Brontë novels, which are the literary ancestors of *Rebecca*.

Hitchcock's luminous, muted technicolor in *The Birds*, like the eerie sunlight of the San Francisco street scenes of *Vertigo* (1958), turns fright and anxiety into strange beauty. Du Maurier's hard-scrabble story, in contrast, seems to have been conceived in harsh black and white: her protagonist is a veteran on a disability pension struggling to support his farm family with part-time work, 'hedging, thatching, repairs'.[3] There may be an echo here of D.H. Lawrence's 'The Fox', with its lesbian homesteaders battling the punishing northern elements. Du Maurier's gruff, proletarian Nat Hocken – who in Hitchcock's version would be transformed into the brash, worldly San Francisco lawyer, Mitchell Brenner – is a painfully isolated consciousness. He alone seems to read the sign language of the birds as they mass: he is as attuned to nature's disturbances as an ancient Druid. The screenplay, written with Hitchcock's usual active collaboration, transfers Hocken's special antagonistic relationship with the birds to a woman who does not exist in du Maurier's story – Melanie Daniels, 'a wealthy, shallow playgirl' (in Hitchcock's words) whose flirtatious games end in her own traumatic humiliation.[4] The screenplay also curiously adds a clinging, manipulative, widowed mother, a theme based on Hitchcock's own early family experience that obsessively runs through his work. Neither sexual intrigue nor Freudian family romance plays any part in du Maurier's stripped-down original conception.

Du Maurier's 'The Birds' may have been suggested by the German air strikes that raked southern England during World War II and that seemed to portend the fall of western civilisation. Boarding up his farmhouse windows against the birds, Hocken recalls the 'air raids' on Plymouth and the 'black-out boards' he made for his mother's house there.[5] Hitchcock picked up the war analogy: of his heroine in *The Birds* becoming stronger through adversity, he said, 'It's like the people in London, during the wartime air raids'.[6] He said the major bird attack at the Brenner house was based on his experience of the London blitz, which had imperilled his own mother: 'The bombs are falling, and the guns are going like hell all over the place. You don't know where to go. … You're caught! You're trapped!'[7]

But nature proves more tyrannous than man. In du Maurier's story, as in the film, the birds invade a child's bedroom with a great 'beating of wings', and a valiant male must go to the rescue, braving 'little stabbing beaks sharp as pointed forks' that draw blood from his hands.[8] In du Maurier's story, the distant city of London, identified with frivolity and political impotence, is horribly overwhelmed by the birds – a motif Hitchcock considered but rejected: he 'toyed with' ending the film with a shot of San Francisco's Golden Gate Bridge 'covered in birds' but decided instead to show the beleaguered family and their guest edging down the driveway past hordes of birds perched on roofs and wires.[9] The dawn rays seem to promise deliverance, something which is missing from du Maurier's finale, where the birds are heard relentlessly, unstoppably splintering the doors.

Both the story and the film keep the reason for the bird attacks mysterious. Du Maurier weaves in agonisingly sporadic BBC reports declaring a 'National Emergency' and speculating that an Arctic air stream has forced the birds south. But Hocken, the man of the country, has immediately perceived the breach in 'nature's law' that normally keeps different bird species from flocking together. The screenplay powerfully shifts this chilling detail to a much later position, where it arouses the scepticism of an elderly woman ornithologist, one of a panoply of vivid cameo characters invented to flesh out the film. Hocken certainly sees malice, concluding after London radio transmissions have ceased that 'many millions of years of memory' stored in the birds' 'little brains' have produced 'this instinct to destroy mankind'. [10] Du Maurier's tale, unlike Hitchcock's, ends in intimations of catastrophe as sweeping as the carnage wrought by Poe's Red Death.

Birds were already present as a sub-theme in Hitchcock's work. In *Blackmail* (1929), his first sound picture, shrill chirping from a bird cage hanging above the heroine's bed gets louder and louder, expressing her sense of entrapment. A bird shop is a nest of conspiracy in *Sabotage* (1936), which climaxes in the delivery of a pair of birds. In *The Lady Vanishes* (1938), birds escape from a crate in a boxcar. In *To Catch a Thief* (1955), Cary Grant sits on a bus between Hitchcock himself and a woman with two green finches fighting in a cage. In *Vertigo*, Kim Novak, posing as Madeleine Elster ('magpie' in German), wears a sharp-beaked gold bird pin on her suit. Birds loom large in *Psycho* (although they did not appear in the original novel on which the film was based): its heroine, Marion, is a Crane from Phoenix, and her murderer, Norman Bates, collects stuffed birds. Cold chicken is eaten in *To Catch a Thief*, and gourmet quail is cooked in *Frenzy* (1972). Fashion parades in Hitchcock often look like feather-flashing bird runs, from the mannequin strut in *The Lodger* (1927) to the garish Louis XV ball in *To Catch a Thief*.[11] At his Jesuit school, the young Hitchcock (who 'did not like eggs' as an adult) 'loved to steal the eggs' from the henhouse and pelt the priests' windows, claiming, 'It looks like the birds have been flying overhead'.[12]

After *Psycho*, Hitchcock had planned to make *Marnie*, which continues *Psycho*'s themes of female theft and mental illness but normalises them with a happy romantic ending. Alas, Grace Kelly's interest in returning to film in *Marnie*'s rather scandalous lead role would eventually be overruled by the grey men of the Monaco bureaucracy. In April of 1960, as he mulled over future projects, Hitchcock saw a newspaper report of an incident in the Southern California town of La Jolla, where a thousand birds flew down a chimney and ravaged the inside of a house.[13] This reminded him of the Daphne du Maurier story, which he had under option but did not think could be developed into a full-scale movie. A year later, however, a far bigger incident in Northern California seized his attention. 'Seabird Invasion Hits Coastal Homes', screamed the headline of the August 18, 1961 *Santa Cruz Sentinel*. Thousands of 'sooty shearwaters, fresh from a feast of anchovies', had flown in from Monterey Bay overnight and smashed into fog-bound coastal areas near Santa Cruz. The gulls, migrating from New Zealand and

South America in flocks numbering in the 'millions', crashed into cars and buildings, broke television aerials and streetlamps, and tried to enter houses when the residents ran out to investigate the noise at 3.0 a.m. – promptly retreating when the birds flew toward the beams of their flashlights.

Hitchcock reacted so quickly to this event, which was covered by reporters from nearby San Francisco, that his name appeared in the initial report in the Santa Cruz newspaper, which ends: 'A phone call came to The Sentinel from mystery producer Alfred Hitchcock from Hollywood, requesting that a Sentinel be sent to him. He has a home in the Santa Cruz mountains.' While the two California incidents were clearly accidental, caused by the birds losing direction and heading for heat in one case and coastal lights in the other, malicious attacks by birds were not unknown. Early the next year, for example, on the same day that one Los Angeles paper reported that, 'after several days' delay caused by hard, cold, continuous and gloomy rain', shooting had begun on Alfred Hitchcock's *The Birds* in Bodega Bay in Northern California, another city paper described how a red-tailed hawk that had attacked small children in Victoria Park had been shot down by local police.[14]

The small town of Bodega Bay, located on the Sonoma coast north of San Francisco, had come to Hitchcock's attention when he filmed *Shadow of a Doubt* (1943) two decades earlier in nearby Santa Rosa. Why was it named after a grocery store ('bodega' in Mexican Spanish), I used to puzzle as I watched *The Birds*? And did the quaint, murky, labyrinthine general store that provides the town's first interior shots have anything to do with the fact that Hitchcock's dictatorial father (who allegedly made the police lock his five-year-old son in a jail cell) had been a greengrocer?[15] As a regional place name, 'Bodega' commemorates the last of the Spanish discoverers in California, Francisco Juan de la Bodega y Cuadro, a Castilian-born captain whose flag ship entered the bay in 1775. His name had been bestowed on an ancestor whom the King of Spain had made overseer of the royal treasure-house ('bodega' once meant 'vault' or 'wine cellar'). The warehouses built by later settlers along the bay were also called 'bodegas'. Hitchcock's use of the peculiarly unforgettable name Bodega Bay has poetic resonance: as a metaphor, 'Bodega Bay', evoking both nature and culture, stands for all of human life.

Hitchcock approached *The Birds* with the documentary naturalism that is the necessary first term of Surrealism – the modernist style to which his work properly belongs and whose pioneers he explicitly acknowledged.[16] He told François Truffaut: 'I had every inhabitant of Bodega Bay – man, woman, and child – photographed for the costume department. The restaurant is an exact copy of the one up there.' The interior of Dan Fawcett's farmhouse is 'an exact replica' of one near Bodega Bay, and 'even the scenery of the mountain that is shown outside the window of the corridor is completely accurate'. The schoolteacher's house combines a schoolteacher's home in San Francisco with one from the bay, because she 'works in Bodega Bay but she comes from San Francisco'.[17] Before the script was written, Hitchcock visited Bodega Bay: 'The whole thing was based on the geography.'[18]

Hitchcock's scholarly attention to the physical world – his pragmatic exactitude and visionary virtuosity, which none of his legion of imitators has understood or been able to duplicate – may have been intensifying in that period. In a memoir about the making of *Psycho*, Janet Leigh describes how Hitchcock had offices and homes in Phoenix extensively photographed, even including a typical young working woman's closet, bureau and suitcases, to ensure the precise realism of Leigh's character, Marion.[19] This exhaustive prior research into externals, which Leigh says was vital to her characterisation, was the polar opposite of the internalising, Stanislavskian 'Method' style of acting that had gained so much prestige since the rise of Marlon Brando that even Marilyn Monroe was making pilgrimages to the Actors' Studio in New York to learn it. As a draughtsman, a Roman Catholic, a gourmand, and a punctilious man of habit, Hitchcock was a ritual formalist who explored psychology not by encouraging his actors to implode in emotional free fall but by containing them within social convention, defined by his strict pictorial frame. 'There is one rule on the set,' Hitchcock told Leigh. 'My camera is absolute.'[20] To Truffaut he said, 'I don't read novels, or any fiction. ... My mind is strictly visual.'[21]

By September 1961, a month after the Santa Cruz incident, Hitchcock, after some vexing false starts, had found a screenwriter, Evan Hunter (author of *The Blackboard Jungle*), with whom he discussed avoiding the lurid science-fiction formulas of 1950s movies. (Two of my favourites from that nuclear-age genre are *Them!* [1954], where giant mutant ants attack Los Angeles, and *Beginning of the End* [1957], in which giant locusts attack Chicago.) But Hitchcock still lacked a leading lady. One October morning a few weeks later, while watching television with his wife and creative consultant, the small, peppery Alma Reville, he spotted a vivacious blonde strolling through a commercial for a diet drink. That afternoon, an appointment was discreetly scheduled with Tippi Hedren, a Minnesota-born model and divorcée who had recently moved from New York to Los Angeles, partly to give her four-year-old daughter, Melanie Griffith (the future actress), a more natural environment to grow up in.

Before she was even screen-tested, Hedren was sent to the Oscar-winning costume designer, Edith Head, whom Hitchcock asked to create a distinctive off-camera look for his new protégée, in much the same way as the moguls of the studio era had commandeered the private and public lives of their contract players. 'That part I found surprising,' Hedren told Donald Spoto. 'He spent as much money on an outright gift of a personal wardrobe as he did on my year's salary.'[22] Hitchcock was actively involved in costuming Hedren for *The Birds*: for example, her expensive gold jewellery was personally chosen by him. 'Hitchcock had a fondness for simple and elegant things like scarves and mink coats,' said Edith Head, 'so these things also became part of her wardrobe.' Because the director sensed in Hedren what Kyle B. Counts calls 'a certain withdrawal, a chaste, cool quality', a suit of 'soft green' was designed for her for the film.[23] Head spoke of Hitchcock's 'very psychological approach to costume' and said of his specifications for Grace Kelly's wardrobe in *Dial M for Murder* (1954), 'There was a reason for every color, every style'.[24] Hitchcock told Hedda Hopper that he painstakingly shaped Eva Marie Saint's look for *North by Northwest*: 'I went along to Bergdorf Goodman's myself and sat with her as the mannequins paraded by. ... I supervised the choice of her wardrobe in every detail – just as Stewart did with Novak in *Vertigo*.'[25]

Tippi Hedren's lavish colour tests cost a then unprecedented $25,000. Two days before they began, Hitchcock's Bellagio Road home in Bel-Air was threatened by the kind of gigantic, devastating brush fire that periodically sweeps through the hills and canyons of Southern California. Ordered to evacuate after 500 other houses were reduced to rubble, the Hitchcocks moved their valuables, including silver, fur coats, and art works, to the wine cellar – the bodega or bunker, which in this case would have proved little protection against nature's fury. Luckily, the fire storm took another path, and after several days in a hotel, the Hitchcocks were permitted to return. For the sedentary director who loved his creature comforts and spoke of his 'passion for orderliness', *The Birds* was clearly born in existential crisis.[26]

Hedren learned she had the role three months later, when the Hitchcocks invited her to dine with them and Lou Wasserman, the head of Universal Pictures, at Chasen's restaurant in Los Angeles. At her place she found a gift box from Gump's (a chic San Francisco store located a few blocks from where the film begins), containing a gold pin of three flying birds studded with seed pearls. After this ritualistic flourish, Hitchcock formally invited Hedren to star in the film – producing tears from her, his wife, and even Wasserman.

Technical preparations for *The Birds* were already under way while Hitchcock was contemplating casting. His first call after the Santa Cruz incident the prior summer had been to Robert Boyle (art director on *Saboteur*, *Shadow of a Doubt* and *North by Northwest*), whom he asked to investigate potential problems in combining live actors with erratic images of mobile birds. Hitchcock initially thought mechanical birds might avoid the distracting shadows that sometimes occur in the standard blue-screen process due to tiny misalignments of the mattes. A bevy of experimental motorised birds, produced at great expense, failed their flight test at Universal and were junked. Cinematographer Robert Burks, a veteran of ten prior Hitchcock films, collaborated with special-effects expert Bud

Hoffman to mix photos of real birds with optical effects in sample footage, which persuaded Hitchcock that this hybrid technique was the way to go.

Boyle also proposed trying an older sodium-vapour process refined by celebrated animation pioneer Ub Iwerks at the Walt Disney studio, where the prism for the process was kept. Hitchcock invited Iwerks, who had just overseen Hayley Mills' wonderful metamorphosis into twins in *The Parent Trap* (1961), to supervise the visual effects of *The Birds*, with the title of special photographic adviser. His first assignment was the scene, based on the La Jolla incident, in which the Brenner living room is invaded by sparrows (actually a mélange of swallows, finches and buntings) who burst from a fireplace. On set, the room was wrapped in polyethylene plastic, which transmitted light but trapped the frantic birds as they were tossed about by air hoses. Quadruple superimpositions were later made on this footage of birds that Iwerks had photographed flying around in a glass booth. The tormented birds would eventually have their revenge by infesting Hitchcock's entire film crew with parasitic lice.

Some fake papier mâché birds made by Lawrence Hampton (credited as special-effects chief) do appear in the film, for example, in Melanie's speeding car and at the children's party. In the fireplace episode, the birds whirling around Mitch's mother, Lydia (Jessica Tandy), are also mechanical, attached by wires running down the actress' neck. A still of this scene, where Lydia bats frantically with both hands at the birds caught in her hair, was so effective that it was used on the movie poster, whose hysterical woman has been universally misidentified (thanks to the retinting of the hair to blonde and the suit to green) as Melanie Daniels. Because screaming makes Tandy's face look strangely younger, the frosty mother and her female rival seem to have physically merged – not unlike *Psycho*'s final fusion of mother and son.

Most of Hitchcock's birds, however, are genuine. He insisted that they be 'domestic birds' and not 'vultures' or raptors.[27] This footage was obtained in ingenious ways. A camera crew took 20,000 feet of film over three days at the San Francisco dump, where they raked garbage into a pile to lure seagulls to dive, perch and feed. To achieve the spectacular 'bird's eye' view of gulls hovering over the burning town of Bodega Bay, a cameraman stood on 'a hundred-foot cliff' on Santa Cruz Island off Santa Barbara while fish were thrown to gulls on the wing.[28] In a 1968 article, Hitchcock described how the rotoscope or travelling-matte process was used for this shot, whereby a single swooping gull was photographically reversed and multiplied. Two women then painstakingly painted in the birds, frame by frame, so that short footage lasting fifteen seconds on the screen took three months to complete.[29]

The crow attack on the schoolhouse contained sixty cuts and required nearly six weeks to assemble. Iwerks engaged L.B. Abbott from 20th Century-Fox to organise this material. Birds photographed in a wind tunnel were optically multiplied and superimposed over film footage of children running on a real Bodega-area road, as well as on a studio treadmill with artificial birds swaying on wires above them. Timing was critical for coordination of the images, and zooming helped ensure perspective. Several trained birds were coached to land on children's necks, but on-screen it's a hand-puppet that bites them.

For the climactic attic scene, where Melanie falls beneath a killer flock, live gulls, crows and ravens were used – to the surprise of Tippi Hedren, who learned only when she arrived on set that day that the mechanical birds had been rejected as unconvincing. Seven days were needed to shoot this horrifying sequence, which takes only two minutes and ten seconds on screen. Hedren called it 'the worst week of my life'.[30] A cage built around the set contained the birds, which were literally thrown at her from a distance of eight to ten feet by prop men wearing padded, elbow-length leather gloves. Periodically, shooting would halt while makeup artist Howard Smit applied latex strips and stage blood to simulate cuts and scratches on Hedren's face and arms. Her hair was tousled, and her green suit gradually ripped. The gull that she whacks with her torch was a dummy, and the real one that bites her hand had a rubber cap fitted over its beak. But the terrorisation of Melanie was also the terrorisation of Tippi, who recalled of the gruelling, day-long operations for the scene's final seconds: 'They had me down on the floor with the birds tied loosely to me through the peck-holes in my dress. Well, one of the birds clawed my eye and that did it; I just sat and cried. It was an incredible physical ordeal.'[31] The injury was a cut to her lower left eyelid.

Was this cavalier treatment of his star sadistic on Hitchcock's part? That Hedren's health and safety were compromised seems obvious. In a state of total collapse, she was forbidden by her doctor to return to work, and so shooting on the film was halted for a week, the first medical emergency on a Hitchcock film in twenty years. 'Torture the women!' Hitchcock once joked, quoting Sardou.[32] In my interview with her, Hedren rejected the widespread theories about Hitchcock's misogynous malice. She said of the attic scene: 'He felt very badly about it. In fact, he couldn't come out of his office until it was really time to roll the cameras.' And of her acquiescence at the time, she remarked, 'This was my first movie, and I didn't know anything. I knew that it took a week to shoot Janet Leigh's shower scene. I thought, well, this is the way it is!'[33] Indeed, Hitchcock himself was uncharacteristically ill at ease throughout production of *The Birds*. Jon Finch, Hitchcock's lead in *Frenzy*, has said, 'He told me that he was terrified of birds. With this film he came into contact with very few actual birds – he always kept his distance from them'.[34]

Iwerks asked Linwood Dunn of Film Effects of Hollywood to help assemble the attic footage. Bob Hoag of MGM was consulted for the harrowing effects in the telephone booth scene at the restaurant. The film's most complex effects, however, were needed for the long final shot, in which the car drives away from the farmhouse under the gaze of what seems to be thousands of birds. Hitchcock called it 'the most difficult single shot I've ever done'.[35] It's a composite of thirty-two images against a matte painting, by pictorial designer Albert Whitlock, of the barnyard, landscape and dawn sky. The barn and moving car required separate segments, as did the foreground, which is in three parts with multiplied photos of the same gulls. Though a third of the birds are fake, there are some live chickens as well as 500 local ducks painted grey. The rustling birds who stir but don't fly as Mitch edges out the porch were either tranquilised or wore 'miniature binders', and the feet of the gulls on rooftops were secured with elastic bands.[36]

Animal trainer Ray Berwick, who had just worked on John Frankenheimer's *Birdman of Alcatraz* (1962), was put in charge of Hitchcock's menagerie. Wild birds proved unexpectedly difficult to catch. Even a nationwide appeal to professional trappers produced none, despite a bounty of $10 per head. Berwick described his night-time stalking of a rookery of 20,000 crows in Arizona, toward which he and an assistant, in 'blackface' and black clothing, had to crawl on hands and knees across a field to throw nets over roosting birds.[37] Berwick needed eight months for preparations and on-set training of his flock, who lived in forty studio pens and consumed 100 pounds of bird seed and 200 pounds of shrimp, anchovies and meat per day.

In the last attack on the Brenner house, we see a close-up not of Rod Taylor's but of Berwick's hand being bitten by a gull, drawing real blood. The bird on the porch that bites Taylor's hand (secretly smeared with meat) is really Berwick's pet crow, Nosey. Admiring the intelligence of the ravens but unimpressed by the gulls, Berwick said, 'The seagulls would deliberately go for your eyes'.[38] During one day alone, a dozen crew members were treated in the hospital for minor flesh wounds from beaks and claws. An inspector from the American Humane Association was always present during production to ensure that the birds were well-treated. After shooting had finished, most were released back to the wild, with the Arizona birds returned to their habitat. However, fifty crows refused to leave the studio lot and perched near Hitchcock's bungalow; they soiled his car until the tree they were roosting in was cut down.

If Berwick was master of nature for the film, the top-flight art design team were arbiters of culture. The first sketches Robert Boyle did for *The Birds*, when it was still set in du Maurier's Cornwall, were based on Edvard Munch's 1893 Symbolist painting, 'The Scream'. Boyle said he was trying to capture 'the sense of bleakness and madness in a kind of wilderness expressing an inner state'.[39] Albert Whitlock, who had worked with Hitchcock in England and would later demolish Los Angeles in *Earthquake* (1974), painted the twelve complex mattes of *The Birds* over a year. He and Boyle toured the Bodega locations to make sketches. The mattes used the natural bay but added buildings, to create a town centre where there was none, and changed the clear marine sky to cloudy – 'to give it mood', as Whitlock put it.[40] The most astounding of the mattes was executed for the aerial panorama of Bodega Bay, which Whitlock filled out with fishing boats, wharves, warehouses and shingled houses. Across the blank middle, footage was superimposed of an actual gasoline fire 'staged', as Hitchcock described it, in a Universal parking lot, with the 'trailing of flaming gas' caught by a camera set up on a hill overlooking the studio.[41] The result is one of the most startlingly memorable shots in the history of film.[42]

Bodega Bay gave Hitchcock the open space and low topography he was looking for to capture the overwhelming effect of birds in flight: the sky would be his monumental canvas. While scouting the area, Whitlock and Boyle identified buildings that could be used in the film. What became the Brenner house was a shack on a 'derelict farm' owned by an eccentric old lady and located on the peninsula of Bodega Head.[43] A new house (since burned down) was built as a shell around the old one; another barn was built closer to the house, a wooden dock laid out, and a gazebo added to the freshly cleared grounds. The nineteenth-century Potter Schoolhouse was located not in Bodega Bay but five miles inland in the town of Bodega, where it still stands. Dilapidated, boarded up, and fated for demolition, it was renovated by Hitchcock's team, who added a jungle gym to the schoolyard. The nearby teacher's house was built from scratch as a temporary façade. The Tides Restaurant, whose interior was reconstructed at the studio, is now long gone, because of the enlargement of the wharf complex. The Fawcett farmhouse remains in private use.

Hitchcock claimed that its state-of-the-art special effects made *The Birds* 'probably the most prodigious job ever done', though many of its composite shots now look rudimentary by the advanced standards of today's dazzling computerised graphics.[44] The film's initial release date of Thanksgiving 1962 had to be postponed to March 1963 due to the complexity of the 412 optical-effects shots, some requiring seven layers of images. Though most of Hitchcock's films were completely cut in advance in his head, as illustrated by his storyboards, there was an unusual amount of excess footage leftover from *The Birds*. Cinematographer Burks and editor George Tomasini had to organise nearly 1,500 shots altogether which, according to Spoto, is 'about twice as many as a normal film, and almost three times as many as Hitchcock ordinarily included'.[45] Embittered scriptwriter Hunter dismissed the ending of *The Birds* as 'that mosaic of 3,407 pieces of film'.[46]

During the months of post-production, Burks ordered the footage to be printed and reprinted by different companies until it met his high standards of realism. Hitchcock also meticulously reconfigured the pleasant California sunshine to get the right look. 'I wanted it to be gloomy,' he said: 'It was necessary to subdue the color of many of the scenes in the film lab to get the proper effect.'[47] Despite these Herculean efforts, *The Birds* did not win the Academy Award for Best Optical Effects, its only nomination. The Oscar went instead to the Elizabeth Taylor epic, *Cleopatra*, which Hitchcock dismissed (along with *Ben-Hur*) as 'nothing' – 'just quantities of people and scenery'.[48]

. . . .

The title sequence of *The Birds*, designed by James S. Pollak, is an avant-garde fantasia in and of itself. Against cold, white, abstract space, black crows flutter back and forth, out of focus as if seen alarmingly too close. There is an eerie continuity from the last shot of Hitchcock's prior film, *Psycho*, where Norman, sunk into psychosis, stares at us as he sits hunched against a blank wall. As *The Birds* begins, we seem to have penetrated into the madman's voracious id, where a blur of animal impulses rave and snap. Against the severity of deep black and blazing white, the titles' very formal, slightly raised classical letters come up in cerulean blue – the lovely pastel of Renoir idylls and romantic hope, of the welcoming robe of merciful Mother Mary, and of the serene, cloudless sky that Hitchcock denies to Bodega Bay. But the hanging words and names nervously overlap and disintegrate, as if bitten to pieces by invisible beaks. The titles show a war between nature and culture, with the irrational and the primitive vanquishing human illusions.

There is no music here or in the film, for the first time in a Hitchcock production since *Lifeboat* (1944), in which a small band of humans also struggle for survival against elemental nature. The only sounds during the credits are the busy flap and flutter of wings, accompanied by raspy, echoing bird cries that subside and then burst out again at the names of the German composers of the pioneering electronic soundtrack, Remi Gassmann and Oskar Sala, with that of Bernard Herrmann, Hitchcock's brilliant musical collaborator, who supervised the sound effects. The bird noise hits a screeching climax at Hitchcock's name: his blue letters also decay, with the fragments swept away by a flurry of wings. Then the screen goes dead black. Does the ear-splitting crescendo mean that Hitchcock is our menacer or the one most menaced? The titles' barbaric attacks on Apollonian colour and form take us on a journey of artistic and psychological regression: Hitchcock, the technicolor master, returns via bleak *Psycho* to the dawn of his film career in black and white – beyond which is the locked prisonhouse of harsh family memory.

After the frightening, introverted white box of the titles – half cosmic void, half mental cage – *The Birds* begins with the happy bustle of everyday life. A bell chimes, as if waking us from a nightmare by a summons to Mass: it's a San Francisco streetcar, packed with mostly male locals and tourists. As it passes, an attractive young woman is seen waiting at the curb. Melanie Daniels, her gleaming, champagne-blonde hair swept up into an elaborate coiffure (recalling Kim Novak's chignon in *Vertigo*), is wearing an elegant, mottled-black ensemble with a tight, very narrow sheath skirt – the only time we see her in anything but the famous pale green suit. The symbolic transition from the titles is subtle but clear: woman is the crow, her stiletto high heels the claws of rapacious nature. Melanie's black leather clutch-bag – evocative term! – is unusually long and lean, like a phallic rifle case.

Behind her is the grand expanse of Union Square, planted with giant, low, broad, clumping palm trees, a lush tropical patch silhouetted against the stony rim of skyscrapers. Briskly crossing the street and turning down the sidewalk toward us, Melanie passes a newsstand travel poster of San Francisco (showing the Golden Gate Bridge of *Vertigo*) and is then stopped in her tracks by a wolf whistle. Half turning with a withering glance to slay the insolent one, she dissolves in a radiant smile when she sees that it is simply a cheeky school boy. Melanie jauntily accepts his homage. Here, remarkably, Hitchcock has exactly restaged the whimsical plot and personae of the television commercial that piqued his interest in Tippi Hedren. (Robert Boyle said of Hitchcock, 'He was quite taken by the way she walked'.)[49] Though she hasn't spoken a word yet, Melanie has already conveyed her character as mistress of chic, a beautiful woman haughtily used to exercising power over men in public and private. As a professional model, Hedren displays a discreet, balletic command in this scene that instantly impressed me as a teenager – as it also did legions of gay men worldwide who have an eye for high fashion. Hedren's Melanie exudes cocky self-confidence and a mesmerising narcissism, prefiguring that of another devastating San Francisco femme fatale played by ex-model Sharon Stone in *Basic Instinct* (1992).

Whirling toward the boy has made Melanie look back over her shoulder toward the plaza. The sound of birds draws her eyes from sidewalk to sky, where masses of seagulls are circling. Her smile fades, and she is frozen with foreboding. Union Square is dominated by the towering Dewey Monument, a nearly one-hundred-foot-tall granite column commemorating Admiral George Dewey's lightning-like naval strike at Manila Bay during the Spanish-American War. It is crowned with a bronze statue of the normally winged Greek goddess Victory, who holds out a laurel wreath in one hand and a trident in the other. [50] Is Victory trying to propitiate the squadrons of restless birds? The bird-woman Melanie will herself be a gift-bearer on her trip to Bodega Bay. And she too will attack by boat in her invasion of the Brenner house. Huge advertising signs over Union Square – 'Air France / Jet to Paris' and 'Jet B.O.A.C.' (British Overseas Airways Corporation) – remind us that mere humans now presume to fly, as if usurping the birds' prerogative. Hitchcock, of course, is our British Airways pilot on this particular flight.

Angled also against the sky is a massive, nineteenth-century iron street lamp, whose fancy twin torches look forward to the attic episode when, besieged like the windblown statue alone and in a high place, Melanie will defend herself against an air raid with a raised torch.

Resuming her errand, Melanie strides into Davidson's Pet Shop, just as Hitchcock himself, appearing in his usual cameo, emerges with his sprightly real-life West Highland White Terriers, Stanley and Geoffrey, prancing ahead on a leash.[51] (As the solemn Hitchcock sweeps with averted face past Hedren, I often think, 'The director abandoning his stars to their travails!') Behind one plate-glass window, marked 'Pets/ Birds/ Tropical Fish', is a very alert, composed cat who turns its head to watch Melanie walk by, as if she were the entertainment. In front of the other window, reversing the positions of audience and performer, a middle-aged couple peruse a tree (like the plaza palms and column) on which pet monkeys clamber (like the men hanging off the streetcar). The wife's hat looks like an inverted flower pot – the first of several assertive hats seen on middle-aged ladies, one clad in a heavy mink stole, who are browsing inside the shop.

These female customers, with their multi-coloured plumage, are the flora and fauna of Hitchcock's Darwinian sexual jungle. Strikingly, the sophisticated Melanie, cutting through the crowd with her bold will and energy, more resembles the dark-suited businessmen striding by, swinging their leather briefcases. Like Ibsen's Hedda Gabler, Melanie takes after her high-ranking father. Hitchcock's animus against more placid, static, fleshy dowagers, coming from his sense of suffocation by his own mother, is overt in *Shadow of a Doubt*, where the charming, amoral anti-hero (Joseph Cotten), graphically describes how such women need murdering, and in *Strangers on a Train* (1951), in which the machiavellian, mother-coddled villain (Robert Walker) nearly strangles an aging socialite at a fancy party.

While the pet shop's exterior was shot on location (the camera was concealed in a furniture-delivery truck), the interior scenes were done on a two-story set at the studio. Trotting up the inside staircase past a forest of aquariums and hanging bird cages, Melanie exclaims to the fussy, stout, elderly Mrs MacGruder, 'Have you ever seen so many gulls? What do you suppose it is?' The shop lady replies, 'There must be a storm at sea. That can drive them inland, you know'. So the film begins with a shared sense of some disturbance in nature. Melanie has a 3 o'clock appointment to pick up an Indian mynah bird, a gift, we later learn, for a respectable aunt whom she means to scandalise with its salty gutter talk. In other words, the rare tropical bird, specifically identified as male, will be capriciously treated as a pawn, a mechanical vehicle of rote, pre-programmed speech. The aunt herself is a hapless stand-in for Melanie's faithless mother, whom her daughter punishes by proxy for abandoning her family. What is not immediately obvious, but can be confirmed by clues such as a wall clock, is that *The Birds* begins at virtually the same moment as *Psycho*, which superimposes across its opening panorama of Phoenix the dateline Friday, 2.43 p.m. (See Appendix: Melanie Daniels' Social Calendar.)

Annoyed and a bit pouty at her delayed order, Melanie leans gracefully over a counter to jot down her address for delivery of the bird. At that moment, Mitchell Brenner (Rod Taylor) arrives, on a parallel mission to buy a gift bird for a female relative, his eleven-year-old sister. Though immediately recognising Melanie as a rambunctious debutante much in the news, he pretends to mistake her for a shop girl (cf. Kim Novak in *Vertigo* as Judy, a real shop girl at Magnin's, where, I suspect, Melanie has just been shopping: it was one block east on Union Square). For a moment before he curtly hails her, we're made to see Mitch's appreciative, somewhat lordly scrutiny of Melanie's rounded bottom and great legs. The latter is a persistent motif in Hitchcock, reflecting his own voyeuristic tastes. In *Saboteur* (1942), the rat-like terrorist (Norman Lloyd) lewdly cases Priscilla Lane's gams on the boat to the Statue of Liberty, but since he is not a gentleman, he coarsely allows her to catch him doing it. As early as *Blackmail*, women's pumps are appreciatively dwelled on as a symbol of the modern (the coquettish heroine is attacked in an attic and wanders in despair past another plaza with a naval monument, Trafalgar Square). Women's bare legs were always shown in the boudoir – as illustrated by Ingres' 'Grand Odalisque' or Manet's 'Olympia' – but never on the street until the 1920s, when Hitchcock was a shy, chubby, still-virgin young adult intimidated by women. A stylish high heel that lengthens the leg and fetishistically arches the foot can be viewed as crippling women and making them more vulnerable, but Hitchcock obviously sees it (as do I) as a formidably sharp weapon of woman's power.

A game is now played between Mitch and Melanie, who goes along with the role of shop girl as she assesses the dashing stranger. His request for 'lovebirds' introduces an explicitly erotic undertone to their exchange, which she accentuates, as she hesitantly improvises her way around the shop, by thoughtfully tapping her pencil on her chin and cheek as artfully as Scarlett O'Hara brandishing her fan at the barbecue in *Gone with the Wind*. The pencil is the Victory trident with which she spears men, as well as the trophy phallus that she knows very well how to grind down. Nearly everything said on both sides in this opening *pas de deux* is a lie: for Hitchcock, deception is intrinsic to love. What I value about this scene, and what I have taken from so many great film-makers,

Melanie masquerading as a shop girl (frame enlargement)

is the way that sexual attraction is shown surging back and forth beneath the level of language (hence my rejection, for example, of rhetorical rubrics like 'No always means no' as useless in the date-rape debate). Words for the keenly visual Hitchcock do not reveal but conceal.

The fencing badinage of this scene, with its thrusts and parries, shows the very structure of courtship in both the human and animal worlds. 'There are different varieties' of lovebirds, Mitch and Melanie agree. This apparently innocuous statement takes in the whole of Hitchcock's oeuvre, from the conventional but illicit or strained heterosexual couplings in *Psycho*, *Young and Innocent* (1937), and *Rebecca* to the homoerotic pairings in *Rope* (1948) and *Strangers on a Train* to the incestuous bondings of mother and son that *Psycho* bequeaths to *The Birds*. Mitch's prudish caveat that birds 'too demonstrative' would be unsuitable for a young girl – a stricture satirically borrowed from his conservative parents' generation – further sexualises the conversation, so that his reference to the 'moulting' season, which Melanie elaborately dubs 'a particularly dangerous time', makes our minds leap from birds losing their feathers to humans shedding their clothes. Hitchcock was so fond of similar double entendres in the picnic repartee in *To Catch a Thief* (where Grace Kelly, unpacking her chicken lunch, offers Cary Grant 'a leg or a breast'), that he made Tippi Hedren re-enact the whole scene in her screen test for *The Birds*.

Despite muffing the names of the caged birds, about whom she plainly knows nothing, Melanie is cool, calm and collected as she flirts with Mitch, her eyes wide and her head appealingly cocked – until, cupped hand out, he demands to inspect a canary. For the first time in the film, Melanie becomes flustered: inexplicably acceding to his unorthodox request, she has lost control of the encounter. Jamming the pencil into her hair – the protruding yellow shaft now becomes his Cupid's arrow, which has struck home and which prefigures the later hit on her forehead – she foolishly opens the cage and puts her hand into it, just as she will later misjudge a risky situation by entering the bird-filled attic. The canary of course escapes, pursued by the now helpless Melanie and frantic shopkeeper, caricatures of addled womanhood. (Structurally, the shopkeeper parallels the aging Lydia, who will also be discomfited by birds loose in the house.) The resourceful male saves the day by nonchalantly clapping his plain, box-like, business hat over the bird when it lights on an ashtray.

'Back in your gilded cage, Melanie Daniels!' Mitch says to the bird (a line Hitchcock added 'during the shooting') as he tucks it back through its door.[52] The game is over, and Melanie is shocked and outraged that she has been bamboozled. If Melanie is the canary, then the hat is the confining institution of marriage that both she and Mitch have avoided. 'Hey, wait a minute!', she barks, and then, 'I think you're a louse'. Her fluted tones and polished manner are gone. Interestingly, as soon as she becomes herself, Melanie behaves like a real shop girl, with the tough, slangy talk of the street. This effect was much more startling in early 1963, since the sexual revolution had not yet begun that would inspire the women of my generation to break middle-class decorum by swearing like sailors.

Mitch, as an attorney at court, once saw Melanie defending herself at a hearing for one of her 'practical jokes that resulted in the smashing of a plate-glass window' (like those of the shop marking the human/ animal borderline). This provides a glimpse of Melanie's madcap life as a hedonistic heiress with a lot of time on her hands. 'The judge should have put you behind bars,' he says flatly, implying that she was treated with undue leniency because of her gender and/or social position. So the canary restored to its cage is doing jail time for her. That broken window will come back to haunt her in the telephone booth, when windows smash on every side of her. And the sound of a window shattering in the major attack at the Brenner house will be as dramatic as the cymbal clash that drowns the assassin's gunshot in *The Man Who Knew Too Much* (1956).

'See you in court!' says Mitch provocatively as he dons his hat with a flourish and saunters out. He has thrown down the gauntlet in sex war. As in Lawrence's *Women in Love*, male and female strive for dominance. The court where Melanie will indeed be punished is the arena of nature: the boat, booth and attic are witness box and execution chamber. But courthouses can also perform civil marriage. Mitch taunts Melanie with the flirtatious bravado of gruff Petruchio wooing 'wildcat' Kate of 'scolding tongue' in *The Taming of the Shrew*.

'Who *was* that man?' the irked Melanie exclaims – as if Mitch were the Lone Ranger galloping out of town. The camera, trained on her, does one of Hitchcock's smooth, subtle zooms, as we are pulled into her inner thought. Suddenly, she bursts into activity and, tottering on her clattering high heels, chases after Mitch down the stairs. Her running, startling the sedate matrons on the first floor, again violates contemporary feminine decorum and begins an enormously long sequence in the film, the stalking of Mitchell Brenner, in which Melanie plays the part of sexual aggressor. Hitchcock lets her flow like a Valkyrie in that energy until the moment when she is hit in the boat by a gull – when sexual control will revert again to Mitch.

This scene, where Melanie scribbles down Mitch's license plate as his car pulls away (to another streetcar chime), is one of my favourite moments in cinema. She grabs a phone and, dialing with the pencil to spare her nails, wheedles a favour (clearly not the first) from the City Desk reporter at the newspaper owned by 'Daddy'. 'Charlie darling, would I try to pressure you?', she purrs seductively, fetchingly toying with the phallic pencil and umbilical telephone cord. Her voice breathy and fake-childlike (listen to the birth of Melanie Griffith in those honeyed vowels!), she uses her feminine charm and family privilege to pirate home-address information from the state's confidential Department of Motor Vehicle files to pay Mitch back for his 'gag' at her expense. She is playing private investigator or police detective, normally a male character in Hitchcock films. (But see the end of *Blackmail*, where policemen hoot derisively, 'We shall soon have lady detectives up at the Yard!' Grace Kelly, as a Melanie-like fashion plate 'who never wears the same dress twice', also pursues zestful crime studies in *Rear Window* [1954].) What I love about this scene is the way it so accurately shows how beautiful women get their way in the world. Men are putty in their hands. When I first saw *The Birds*, blonde sorority queens ruled social life in most American high schools, a tyranny I accepted as their divine due. Melanie Daniels has the arrogant sense of entitlement of all beautiful people who sail to the top, from Athenian stoa and Florentine court to Parisian salon and New York disco. Nature gives to them, but then nature takes away.

'Do you have any lovebirds?', Melanie calls out to the shopkeeper, who in post-menopausal detachment has hovered half-baffled at the edge of these charged manœuvres. The scene ends with Melanie lost in conspiratorial thought, her eyes mischievously darting and her face glowing with autoerotic glee. There is an amusing, crisp cut to the much-sought lovebirds in their cage, as Melanie carries it through the front door of Mitch's apartment building the next morning. We see only her brown pumps and color-coordinated purse and gloves, as well as the heavy skirt of her luxurious, full-length, beige mink coat. As she steps into the elevator, the camera pans up the plain blue suit of a curious passenger (Richard Deacon), then follows his appraising gaze sideways to Melanie's vacantly smiling, superciliously tilted face. Hitchcock dwells on the contrast between the businessman's sober uniform and the gorgeous plumage of the human female on parade – the exact reverse of the animal world, where the male displays and the female needs dull camouflage to protect her young from predators. Hitchcock savours the mystique of sexual differentiation: he knows that the sexes, despite their socialised overlap, permanently diverge at their natural extreme.

Melanie's costume change is significant. Yesterday, as a maverick bachelor girl, she was in austere, wintry black: her tailored bolero jacket, with long black gloves under three-quarter-length sleeves, had a mandarin collar reminiscent of a priest's cassock (as worn by Montgomery Clift in Hitchcock's *I Confess* [1953]). Today, on her romantic mission, she is in spring colours of light brown and pastel green, as if she were signalling œstrus, the promise of fertility. Furthermore, her green suit is color-coordinated with the parrot-like green lovebirds, who are capped with a splash of vermilion. She too will be christened with blood-red in the boat in Bodega Bay. Her opulent fur symbolises human dominion over nature as well as male economic power in society. From earliest history, fur and jewellery have been trophies heaped by men on women in tribute to their beauty. Pampered and parasitic, Melanie is an exquisite artifact of high civilisation. She is literally a walking work of art.

Indifferent to their care, Melanie deposits the birds with a note outside Mitch's door, as if they were bait in a mantrap. The nosy neighbour must officiously warn her that Mitch is away for the weekend. She snaps out of her sexy haze and turns all business. The man, giving her an even franker once-over than in the elevator, indiscreetly blabs the details of Mitch's private life and habits – his weekend trips to see his family in Bodega Bay, including the distance ('60 miles north' – a bit exaggerated) and choice of roads. It's as if the spell of sexual attraction automatically suspends the rules of ethics.

The next quick cut is again to the lovebirds in transit, as their cage rests on the passenger-side floor of Melanie's sports car, an expensive and very rare Aston-Martin convertible. They are swaying side by side on their perch as she speeds along the longer, winding, scenic coastal highway. It's always amusing because the birds seem so patient and attentive, though they see nothing of the picturesque rocky landscape.

For the moment, they are Melanie's pets (like Hitchcock's dogs), and they oscillate loyally in sync with her by centrifugal force. We see them juxtaposed with Melanie's pointed shoe pressing the accelerator – again showing Hitchcock's delectation in high heels as well as his frisson at woman literally putting her foot down.

We must note the aggressive pleasure with which Melanie deftly accelerates through the curves at top speed with the wind hitting her face and rippling the gauzy chiffon scarf around her hair. Grace Kelly in *To Catch a Thief* is also a flamboyant driver, giving Cary Grant a careening, white-knuckle ride along the same Corniche on which the future Princess of Monaco would be killed in a mysterious one-car accident. But Melanie Daniels is free as a bird: she rides alone, amused by her own meddlesome thoughts and plans. Tippi Hedren is terrific as she shifts gears and rests her fawn-gloved hands on the steering wheel. What could be more representative of modern female liberation than an elegantly dressed woman gunning a roadster through the open countryside? Aerial views of the car on the deserted road dramatise Melanie's independence and pluck. Before the debut of the Ford Mustang in 1964, it was primarily men who enjoyed the prerogative of the sports car (as in Martin Milner and George Maharis in their white Corvette in the hit television series, *Route 66*), so this scene was daring and exhilarating. Robin Wood rightly compares Melanie's drive to Bodega Bay with Marion's to the Bates Motel in *Psycho*.[53] But Marion is a nervous driver overwhelmed, to her misfortune, by a rainstorm. She has Hitchcock's own anxieties about driving, which he refused to learn – to avoid, he claimed, being ticketed by the feared police (cf. *Psycho*'s looming roadside officer). Unlike Marion, whom we see in flight, Melanie drives as a vivacious expression of her combative personality. She's more like Germaine, Cary Grant's portly housekeeper in *To Catch a Thief*, who 'strangled a German general' with her bare hands and leads the French police on a wild car chase through the Riviera hills.

In her superb book on the soundtracks to Hitchcock's movies, Elizabeth Weis analyses the 'great reliance on sound effects' in the otherwise scoreless *The Birds* and finds this 'a logical outgrowth of Hitchcock's creative development' in *Psycho*, where Bernard Herrmann's screeching violins at Marion's murder mimic Norman's birds. Lauding Hitchcock's habit of 'separating sound and image', she points out, 'During a Hitchcock film we are typically looking at one thing or person while listening to another'.[54] Applying this to Melanie's drive to Bodega Bay, we can appreciate how we are made to hear her car before we locate it streaking through the vast panorama. The screeching tyres convey her addiction to thrills. Weis calls Melanie's grinding gears 'mechanical noises', showing that she herself is 'cold and mechanical'. I would modify this slightly: Melanie, like D.H. Lawrence's Nietzschean industrialist, Gerald Crich, treats people and situations as if they were mechanical.

The air view of Bodega Bay, with its boat-dotted harbour, rolling, green meadows, and grazing cows, is as tranquil as a Constable painting. Arriving by picturesque detour via Bay Hill Road, Melanie's silver-blue car coasts into the town centre and pulls up with a roar, as pedestrians turn and stare.[55] She's conspicuously out of place in this working fishing village, with its bulky, dated vehicles.[56] Her first stop is Brinkmayer's general store, which sells groceries and hardware, issues dog licenses, and serves as the post office. Thus the main parts of *The Birds* both begin in shops, which Hitchcock treats as curio-filled cultural institutions equivalent to the British Museum seen in *Blackmail*. We hear another chiming bell (echoes of Hitchcock's Jesuit education?) as Melanie opens

the door of the cluttered shop and steps inside. With her lavish fur coat, she's like a dream vision, a golden goddess who has descended in her sky-blue chariot to earth. The grand-fatherly shopkeeper (who, in a major gaffe, speaks with a Vermont accent belonging to *The Trouble with Harry* [1955]) is first gruff and laconic, then slowly, bashfully bewitched, gazing at her like the elders of Troy thunderstruck by matchless Helen, for whom they think the city well lost. Melanie turns detective again, grilling the man about Mitch's address. When he points out the Brenner house

The shopkeeper points out the Brenner house across Bodega Bay across the bay ('See them two big trees?' – the Golgotha where she will be nailed), she is dismayed to hear him refer to Lydia Brenner and 'the two kids' – implying that Mitch is already married. But no, the 'kids' are Mitch and his sister: though nearly a generation apart, they are locally collapsed together, suggesting that Mitch, tied to his mother, is still partly trapped in childhood.

When Melanie decides, on a whim, to surprise Mitch by boat, the shopkeeper sceptically asks, 'Did you ever handle an outboard boat?' She breezily replies, 'Oh, of course!' As he obligingly phones for a boat to be brought to the wharf, a dispute breaks out over the name of the little Brenner girl; he calls back and forth to a gravelly, hilariously disembodied, frog-like male voice in the back room: 'Alice, isn't it?' 'No, it's Lois.' They're both wrong. Names are uncertain and shifting – just as in the film's disintegrating titles. Both shop scenes, in San Francisco and Bodega Bay, contain misidentifications of birds or women, which the film often ominously treats as a single category of capricious being. Both scenes, ending in a free phone call asking for a favour, show how Melanie is royally accustomed to being helped, supported and served by men. As the shopkeeper stands with phone in hand, Melanie waits near a shelf of conch shells, whose pink genitalia at her ear may be humming with nature's own messages. So she too is on the phone – to Venus?

The shopkeeper sends her to a higher authority: Annie Hayworth, the schoolteacher as oracle. Melanie leaves the strange establishment, which is as spatially jumbled as the knitting sheep's dark shop in Lewis Carroll's *Through the Looking-Glass* (which similarly metamorphoses into a rowboat), and drives up the road toward Annie's house. She pauses in front of the old Victorian schoolhouse that looms up like the spooky Bates mansion in *Psycho* (whose ornate Gothic style Hitchcock described as 'California gingerbread').[57] Over the door is a sign in large letters: 'BODEGA BAY SCHOOL'. At this point in the film, I customarily intone aloud, 'We all go to school in Bodega Bay!' It is my Nicene Creed, by which I affirm the overwhelming power of pagan nature.

Zooming off with spinning wheels and a burst of flying gravel, Melanie pulls up to Annie's picket fence. She sprints up to the porch, rings another bell, and hears yet another disembodied voice, Annie calling out 'Who is it?' from the garden, where she has been digging. 'Me,' Melanie replies with childish solipsism, as if back in the schoolroom. The teacher appears with smudged face to offer a cigarette from a crumpled pack – as if soldier-to-soldier in the sexual trenches. Suzanne Pleshette plays Annie with wonderful ironic insouciance and world-weariness. 'This tilling of the soil can become compulsive,' she drawls – a bit like fag-puffing Billie Whitelaw ('the thinking man's Venus') grumpily dragging herself out of bed to offer Albert Finney a chemical-free farm breakfast in *Charlie Bubbles* (1968). In tone and vocabulary (cf. the Freudian 'compulsive'), Annie immediately conveys that she is a sophisticated urbanite marooned in Bodega Bay. Even if her mannish, nondescript grey slacks and sneakers suggest that she's going to seed, her vivid red sweater and mailbox (stencilled with the screen-siren name 'Hayworth') advertise her vibrant female sexuality – more natural and intense than that of the cool, game-playing Melanie.

The delicate permuations of mutual scrutiny, wary curiosity, and burgeoning competitiveness between the brunette Annie and the blonde Melanie are brilliantly captured by Pleshette and Hedren. When I fervently praised their remarkable scenes, Tippi Hedren surprisingly replied, 'You're one of the first people that have really said *anything* about it'. Of working with the then relatively unknown Pleshette (whom Hitchcock had also seen on TV), she said: 'We had a *wonderful* time together! It was interesting to play those little scenes, which had to be very tense. It was very tricky.'

'Are you a friend of Mitch's?', Annie pointedly asks, after divulging the real name of his sister, Cathy, and sardonically impugning the town's male-run mail service. So detective work now begins on Annie's part, and she misses nothing. As in the pet shop scene, the script cannot convey what the camera does, showing in Annie's subtle changes of expression the fierce currents beneath the surface of casual conversation. Hitchcock is recording the same machinations and jockeying for territory that Oscar Wilde wittily exaggerates in the tea-table scene of *The Importance of Being Earnest*, where Gwendolyn and Cecily are at loggerheads over a will-o'-the-wisp fiancé. Hitchcock shows how sexual power, mediated as it may be through social forms, ultimately springs from the natural will to power. His women always have both craft and instinct.

The lovebirds cheep when Annie leans into the car: are they registering, like geiger counters, her own buried love for Mitch or giving early warning of her demise two days later on this very walk? Annie instantly understands the import of the gift: 'Good luck, Miss Daniels,' she says with courtly formality. Melanie accepts this with equal, archaic formality and grandly sweeps away in her car like a mounted knight off to try his luck in wooing the princess of the castle. At this moment, the desirable male has shrunk to but one item on the female sexual agenda.

Armed with the covert intelligence she needs, Melanie returns to town and, in a series of deft Hitchcock cuts, uses the hood of her car to write (with her left hand) a clearly just-purchased card to Cathy, then drives down to the wharf to pick up her boat. Greeted by distant, warning bird cries, she parks next to a turquoise pickup truck that entered the middle distance when she first gazed across the bay at the Brenner house: it resembles but does not actually appear to be Lydia Brenner's Ford truck. Nevertheless, the juxtaposition of car and truck suggests the two women are in parallel orbit. Bird cage in hand, Melanie turns two workmen's heads as she hurries past a row of crab traps – reminding us that she too is a fisher of men. As she chats with the weatherbeaten boatman in his watch cap (like Hitchcock's own forebears, who were fishermen), we see the names of several yachts in the marina, notably 'Frolic', which describes Melanie's cavalier attitude toward life. Two others ('Maria' and 'Donna', as in Madonna?) are female, in the traditional allegory of the sea that personified vessels as 'she'.

The baffled boatman, shaking his head, helps Melanie down the wooden ladder to the small boat and hands her the bird cage, as if he were a footman settling a lady in her carriage and handing in her muff. He effortlessly starts the motor and watches her nonchalantly putt off. When I asked Hedren whether she had any prior experience with outboard motors, she replied, laughing, 'Never before!' When asked the same question by the production staff during filming, she says she borrowed Melanie's line from the general store: '"Of course!" I just mimicked what was in the script. I had to *fake* it!'

The location photography of Melanie crossing Bodega Bay is of high-art quality. We see her in profile, as the boat cuts like a shark fin across the still water, and then in full face, with the distant town behind her, the schoolhouse dominating it and far larger than any church. (God plays no role in this film or in du Maurier's original story.) In the eerie, artificially subdued light, Melanie glides on her mission with preternatural ease. A woman in a fur coat with a bird cage in a rowboat: it could be a Surrealist painting by Dali or Magritte. The scene is hypnotically unsettling in archetypal terms. On the smooth waters, Melanie is like the Lady of the Lake or those sinister, self-contained femmes fatales who go boating – Spenser's Acrasia, Shelley's Witch of Atlas, or Gene Tierney as a psychopathic murderess in sunglasses in *Leave Her to Heaven* (1945). Hedren at the helm exudes an airy, affable elitism, a noble, relaxed power, like the banqueting Olympians of the Elgin marbles.

As she hoves within sight of the Brenner homestead, Melanie cuts the motor and scrutinises the activity onshore, where Mitch is bidding goodbye to his mother and sister, who drive off to town in the turquoise pickup truck. When he walks off toward the barn, Melanie paddles in (with an oddly convenient canoe paddle rather than a more logical but unwieldy oar). Though the theme is romantic intrigue, the imagery is of warfare. She is like the rangers who came ashore under fire on D-Day and scaled the Normandy cliffs. Pulling up to the dock, she throws the looped hawser over the stanchion, which in a Hitchcock film (strangulation always being a leitmotif) ends up looking like a hangman's noose lassoing a penis. Stealthily carrying the cage down the dock toward the house, she could be a terrorist planting a bomb.[58] She is primly never without her alligator-leather purse – the kind of strapped, pyramidal, snap catch-bag that Hedren will sport in the train-platform opening of *Marnie*, where the convoluted, yellow leather end-folds are so lingered on by Hitchcock's camera that they turn vulval. *Marnie*'s purse (the term 'alligator purse' occurs in a Baltimore children's song) is both the voracious mother and the locked psyche of the sex-phobic heroine. The purse of *The Birds* is a hunt bag in which to stuff male quarry. Like William Blake in 'The Crystal Cabinet', Hitchcock portrays the vagina as a male jail.

Tiptoeing into the house, Melanie is trespasser and burglar – but one who leaves something rather than steals it. She does not, of course, ring the doorbell, just as she silently baited Mitch's door in town. The birthday gift of lovebirds, left for Cathy with a perplexing note from a total stranger, is not as benign as it looks. First of all, Melanie is 'marking' violated territory, like a male dog watering another's turf, which is here strongly matriarchal: she glamourously cuts through the modest, stuffy, early American interior like the lord of the manor at a serf's cottage. Second, Melanie is using a child, as much as she uses the birds, as a tool to get to Mitch. Third, she is coercing and manipulating him, forestalling resentment of her stalking him by diverting him with gratitude for her generosity to his sister. It's a form of emotional blackmail. Fourth, in plot terms, it is Melanie who introduces or rather smuggles the first birds into a building – as if they were microbes that will become a 'plague'(a word used later by Mitch). Indeed, when she tears up her note to Mitch and sets up Cathy's, one lovebird expresses its irritation by nipping at it.

There's a great shot of Melanie running back down the dock, as the camera follows her on its briefly visible track. I adore it when she pushes off by thrusting her paddle against the pilings. Hedren plays it with all the lithe physicality and verve of the great screwball comedy heroines of the 30s, from Carol Lombard to Katharine Hepburn, who were always playing irrepressible heiresses.[59] Taking the boat out a bit, she gleefuly lies face down – heedless of her fur coat – to spy on developments. What a reversal of sex roles: shell bag at the ready, she is the hunkered-down hunter, skulking in a duck blind, while the male is her prey. Meanwhile, Mitch runs back and forth onshore after finding the birds in the house. The recumbent Melanie could be aiming a shotgun at a zigzagging rabbit.

When he catches sight of the boat, she sits up and tries to start the motor. It takes six yanks to do it, and the hacking, hesitating sputters may suggest that her penetration and control of the physical world are about to end. Indeed, at this moment, squawking gulls fly for the first time into the frame. Mitch dashes back into the house and emerges with binoculars – for battle or bird-watching. Recognising her, he smiles with pleasure. She beams with triumph and arch self-satisfaction, steering the boat straight back toward town. This scene always reminds me of that moment when Carroll's Alice, sitting in a train compartment with a talking goat and a gentleman dressed in white paper, is inspected by a guard through a telescope, a microscope, and opera-glasses. Mitch, pulling Melanie into focus, is like Hitch the director, baffled and bemused by women and contemplating them across the wide wastes of gender.

Leaping into the car by which she trailed him, Mitch speeds and splashes along the road arcing around the bay. It's a race between male and female – the kind of mixed-gender contest that has unfortunately fallen out of favour (except for Billie Jean King's trouncing of a geriatric Bobby Riggs) since the days of Atalanta. Melanie is gliding so fast, she seems to fly – like a cormorant skimming the water. Mitch, who is wearing a white fisherman's sweater and a dapper blue ascot (named after the British race track), beats her to the wharf and, hand on hip, waits for her with blasé, macho delight. At this moment, Melanie is at the height of her power, like Cleopatra sailing into the Cydnus on her barge. She wears an ambiguous, mocking Mona Lisa smile, her coral lipstick sparkling like pink diamonds. By ambush and provocation, she feels she has the upper hand. But the air and water, grey-green dappled with violet as in Manet, have turned perceptibly darker.

Just as Melanie cocks her head and gives a geisha-like moue of florid flirtation, a gull dives into the frame and slams her in the head. It's grotesquely shocking, no matter how many times one has seen the film. Nature and culture collide. The gull's blow is first shot in what the lady ornithologist will later call 'the bird war'. Hitchcock has wonderfully choreographed it, so that as Melanie gasps (the bird's cry seems to speak for her), her right hand flies to her forehead while she makes a spasmodic, angular motion with her raised left arm that is half-kabuki, half-Martha Graham. The whole thing has the asymmetrical beauty of a chance gesture in Degas. The blow causes a collapse of social forms, like the portentous, grinding fracture of the stone baluster in *Last Year at Marienbad* (1961).

Next, Melanie inspects her palm in horror, with a look of complex thought on her face, as if she were reading a letter with dreadful news. Finally, there's a close-up of her now-soiled, suede-gloved fingers, with a crimson splotch of blood on the index tip – a Surrealist reversal of her lacquered red fingernails. She resembles the sleepwalking Lady Macbeth ('Out, damned spot!') facing her moral culpability, as well as the sex-tortured hero of Luis Buñuel's and Salvador Dali's *Le Chien andalou* (1928), transfixed by ants (uncontrollable desires) running all over his palm. Archetypally, the shot is a *memento mori*: as if looking into a mirror, the painted socialite sees the skull beneath the skin and counts the blood-price of woman's romantic games. The crimson circle staining her glove also recalls Kim Novak's black-gloved finger eerily probing the sequoia circles of *Vertigo*: 'Here I was born, and there I died,' Madeleine says, as if charting her transmigrating soul.

Though this scene was partly filmed on the water in Bodega Bay, Melanie's close-ups were done in the studio. Her wounding required special ingenuity. Hedren told an interviewer:

Up in the rafters they had a wire on a slope and, on top of it, a dummy sea gull. A tube was run from a sort of bicycle pump through my dress. The hairdresser then did my hair, spraying it very tightly except for one little piece in front, which is where the end of the tube came. They synchronized it with footage of a gull shot at the San Francisco garbage dump so that when they let go of the dummy bird to swoop down at me, they hit the pump, which blew my hair up, and it looked as if the gull had actually hit me. At the same time a trickle of blood was released to create the illusion that I'd been cut. I thought it was very clever.[60]

The blood exquisitely trickling down Hedren's forehead is a martyr-like, early motif in Hitchcock, occurring on men in *Young and Innocent* and *Number 17* (1932) and on a sexy blonde (Madeleine Carroll) in a train wreck in *Secret Agent* (1936). I suspect it was inspired by the blood dripping from the hero's mouth in the same dream sequence of *Le Chien andalou*. In *The Birds*, combined with Melanie's haute couture and glistening *maquillage*, the blood has a sadomasochistic sensuality. The man-vanquishing expression on her face just before the gull strikes replicates Grace Kelly's inviting look as she surprises Cary Grant with a steamy, hotel corridor kiss in *To Catch a Thief*.

Why is Melanie punished? Is the bird's attack a random event or an act of karmic justice? Hitchcock said Melanie 'represents complacency – smug complacency'.[61] He told Peter Bogdanovich, 'This girl, who is just a fly-by-night, a playgirl, comes up against reality for the first time'.[62] Interviewing Hitchcock, François Truffaut compared Melanie to the hardbitten journalist of *Lifeboat*, Constance Porter (Tallulah Bankhead), 'starting out as a jaded sophisticate and, in the course of her physical ordeal, gradually becoming more natural and humane', accompanied by 'the discarding of purely material objects', like her typewriter and diamond bracelet.[63] Indeed, imagistically, Melanie Daniels in her fur coat in the rowboat is a recasting of Constance in her 40s, square-shouldered, dark-brown mink coat, casually smoking with legs crossed in the lifeboat, amid floating debris of a shipwreck. Constance has Melanie's ironic detachment but not her mechanical aptitude: it's the men who row and labour in *Lifeboat*. Hitchcock is upgrading the female athleticism: by *Marnie*, his heroine (like the one in *Jamaica Inn*) will be riding and jumping horses.

38   Mitch comes to Melanie's aid after she is hit by the gull

However, though Constance may be 'stripped', as she puts it, of her 'worldly possessions', she exits her film with mental clarity intact. Melanie, ironically, ends up like *Lifeboat*'s shellshocked young mother around whom Constance drapes her mink coat – lost when the woman, distraught at her baby's death, slips over the side to drown herself.

In the crisis of the gull attack, Mitch and Melanie drop their masks of combative flirtation: extremity unites them in common cause, as the flesh proves too, too frail. Stunned, Melanie is totally helpless and, as at the bird shop, must be rescued by a male. Rod Taylor, showing off the rugged muscularity that had already captivated my generation of girls in *The Time Machine* (1960), leaps acrobatically in several, sharp synchronised moves off the wharf, onto the pilings, and into the boat to pull it in and help Melanie out. She is rather prettily half-reclining with legs extended, which the camera captures by a nice elevated shot. He is definitely more masculine now than she, doing things that she can't in high heels. And his quick, clambering swings recall the monkeys in the shop window. The scene resembles one in *Vertigo* where James Stewart leaps into another bay to save Madeleine at the Golden Gate Bridge.

'That's the damnedest thing I ever saw! It seemed to swoop down at you deliberately!', Mitch cries, introducing the theme of nature's demonic malevolence. 'That's the girl,' Mitch urges Melanie, as she gingerly ascends the ladder – perhaps the first step in her regression to childhood. When he counsels a tetanus shot, Melanie has regained enough composure to say she had 'a booster' before going abroad last May, which helps fill in the chronology of her recent, fun-filled life. They find the door locked at the marina office. 'Out to Lunch', a sign says, marking the time of day for us as the plot progresses. Continuing up the path, they pass the telephone booth (which will calamitously recur), as well as a painted wall sign: 'Sea Food Restaurant'. Subliminally, we may realise that the seagull too went out for lunch and that Melanie was it.

Heads turn again as Mitch guides the unsteady Melanie into the busy Tides Restaurant. He calls for antiseptic from the hovering owner, who's concerned mainly about liability for injuries occurring on his premises: this legal theme makes Melanie realise Mitch is a lawyer. 'Is that why you want to see everyone behind bars?', she prods him. He solicitously dabs the antiseptic on her forehead, going on and on with it until the movement becomes peck, peck, peck – like the crow that will later drum on the head of a flattened schoolgirl. It's a moment of stolen intimacy in the noisy public space of the diner. The camera holds very tight on Mitch and Melanie and even turns at a slight (north-by-northwest!) angle to highlight their developing relationship. Whereas at their first meeting he dared her to stick her hand into a cage, here he is in a caretaking, almost nurse-like role, as with his widowed mother.

What I particularly love about this scene is that the waitress (the bouncy Elizabeth Wilson in an early bit part as the owner's wife) brings a bottle of peroxide from the diner's rudimentary medical kit. It is this that Mitch holds in his hand like a magic elixir and applies with a cotton swab to Melanie's wound. As a bottle blonde herself, she seems to gain strength from the peroxide, which operates on her like a transfusion of plasma. The dye theme appears in Hitchcock as early as *The Lodger*, where a serial murderer is stalking blondes: a young woman exclaims at the news, 'He killed another fair-haired girl. No more peroxide for yours truly!' Hitchcock treats blonde as a beautiful, false colour, symbolising women's lack of fidelity and trustworthiness. Melanie seems to soak up the peroxide just as the injured seaman (William Bendix) of *Lifeboat* quaffs courage from Constance's silver-and-glass flask of brandy. One touch of peroxide restarts Melanie's games ('I loathe you,' she taunts Mitch with drawling erotic provocation), as well as her lies (she spins a tale of knowing Annie Hayworth from schooldays). Hitchcock has jokingly seated Melanie beneath a sign that says 'Packaged Goods Sold Here', which turns her into a Dionysian liqueur (Lacrimae Christi?) or a fancy, high-priced courtesan (cf. 'Don't squeeze the goods' in *Frenzy* and 'She's a neat piece' in *Jamaica Inn*).

The amiable sparring between Mitch and Melanie intensifies until he becomes a tough attorney cross-examining a slippery witness in court. Just as Melanie, falsely denying she came to Bodega Bay to see him, declares, 'I can't say I like your seagulls much either,' the diner door opens, and there's Mitch's mother, the town's chief carnivorous bird. The two women size each other up, in a darker, fiercer replay of the Annie–Melanie encounter. Mitch's car parked near the wharf has caught his mother's attention: so she too, like Melanie, has tracked him down via his vehicle. Wood asserts that Lydia and Melanie 'look remarkably alike', with 'similar upswept hairstyles', and that Lydia is Melanie 'as she will look in thirty years' time'.[64] But as a sober matron, Lydia is wearing a plain, salt-and-pepper (like her hair) cloth coat with a clay-brown scarf that doesn't really match. Wood notes that Lydia, at mention of the lovebirds, repeats Annie's line ('Oh, I see', a refrain in the script) to signal her discovery of Melanie's single-minded romantic mission. As if following Melanie's peroxide-fuelled precedent, Mitch tells a bald social lie, rather rudely putting his mother on the spot by claiming he's already invited Melanie to dinner. The tension is enormous. Mitch mischievously grins like the Cheshire Cat, while the women bristle like tigers. Miffed at Lydia's frostiness, Melanie digs in her heels and refuses to let Mitch pick her up for dinner: 'I can find my own way,' she says, in what could stand as a manifesto of feminist independence.

Such scenes, prickly with unexpressed hostility, show Hitchcock's enormous artistry. It's a war to the death in a public place, but nothing shows beyond this tight circle of three. The flick of an eyelid, the subtlest change of mood, an infinitesimally less-than-enthusiastic reply: Hitchcock, in real life a notorious raconteur and monologuist, obviously had an uncanny ability to observe and soak up reactions, the nonverbal cues that give his great films such psychological power.

We fade from Lydia's pensive face (dissolving like the titles) to Annie's house, where Melanie is again mounting the porch and ringing the bell (with her thumb). She furtively smooths her hair in the glass door to refurbish her persona after the incident in the bay. When she appears, Annie literally stands in the door as if barring the way and, as if compensating for her dowdiness earlier in the day, leans like an Amazonian ship's figurehead with pointed bust aggressively thrust toward Melanie. Indeed, she advances with such air-buffeting momentum that Melanie actually takes a step backward! After leaving the diner, Melanie has gone to the general store and bought, we later learn, a prim flannel nightgown, which she is toting like a school lunch in a brown paper bag (cf. the 'yards of brown paper' on which Hitchcock charted the film's plot).[65] She comes as a suppliant to Annie, who has a 'Room for Rent' sign in her window – just like the sign that attracts the mysterious, vampiric stranger in *The Lodger*. Melanie claims the hotels in town are full – unlikely during the chilly season? – and asks to rent the room for one night. Annie resists but relents, laughing at Melanie's rumpled, make-do valise ('It's utilitarian!' – another highfalutin word). Like Cary Grant's Roger Thornhill in *North by Northwest*, Melanie is travelling without luggage and has been overdressed for her gritty outdoor adventures.

As Melanie is about to cross Annie's threshold for the first time, we hear distant bird cries. Annie looks up, her smile fading. 'Don't they ever stop migrating?' she asks with disgust. It's as if, alone and sexually frustrated, she is fatigued by Mother Nature's instinctual imperatives. There's a cut to the blue sky, framed by her self-confining porch, crossed by dozens of white gulls. Melanie whirls to look up, repeating her worried gaze at the bird-filled sky over Union Square. The scene ends on the still, silent women's foreboding faces staring upward. In the film, Melanie herself is a migrating bird who, like the cuckoo, invades and usurps others' nests. Indeed, in *The Lodger*, Hitchcock focuses on a furiously chiming cuckoo clock as the hawk-nosed new tenant passes, like huntress Melanie, through a shadowy front door.

The next shot shows Melanie's car pulling into the Brenner barnyard with a circular flourish. Now that she has arrived openly by car rather than by boat, we get a long view of the road, telephone wires, and receding hills that will reappear, blanketed with birds, at film's end. Making another nervous backstage gesture at arrival, Melanie touches up her lipstick in a compact, as we examine every angle of her perfect, Marie Antoinette coiffure; a few bird cries seem to signal disapproval. When she rings the bell (as she did not on her morning sortie to the house), there is no answer – prefiguring Lydia's visit to the still-as-death Fawcett farmhouse. The three Brenners appear walking from the barn, where they have been brooding about the chickens. Mitch waves, while young Cathy (Veronica Cartwright) breaks from the pack and dashes up to fling her arms around Melanie. Her effusiveness, inspired by the lovebirds, is in marked contrast to her mother's grudging behaviour: Lydia does not greet and only thinly smiles at Melanie, the interloper. 'Is there a man and a woman? I can't tell which is which!', the innocently prepubescent Cathy chatters about the birds, while the camera lingers on Lydia's cold, appraising face, which shows the battle fatigue and stalemate of sex war as much as did Annie's in the prior scene.[66] 'The chickens won't eat,' Mitch confides to Melanie. In genuine hospitality, food symbolises something greater: tonight, Lydia may physically feed her guest, but she will starve her emotionally.

As they enter the house, Lydia neither welcomes Melanie nor invites her to take off her coat but makes a beeline for the telephone to call the owner of the general store to complain about chicken feed. Lydia assumes fraud. '*Caveat emptor*, Mother – let the buyer beware!', Mitch calls out as, unwrapping the posh package at hand, he chivalrously helps Melanie with her voluminous coat. 'Whose side are you on?', Lydia replies – a challenge equally applying to her female rivalry for her son's affections. As she wrangles with Fred Brinkmayer (whom she's harassing at home; it's afterhours), Mitch chats with Melanie in the background and mixes her a drink. We hear Melanie ask, 'Is that your father?', about the large, framed, colour photograph over the piano.

Lydia slowly becomes less self-assured as her phone call goes on. Learning that the Fawcett chickens also won't eat, even though it's different feed, she asks, 'You don't think there's something going around, do you?' – meaning a communicable disease. But of course Melanie herself is what's really going around Bodega Bay! Jessica Tandy, as Lydia, shows wonderful skill in executing this one-sided phone conversation in a single, long, stately take: her voice traverses an amazing range of rhythm, intonation and dynamics. Contemporary actors seem to have lost the ability to make such basic bits of stage business interesting or compelling.

Oddly, we skip the dinner itself and cut directly to the clean-up afterward – as if food doesn't exist as a concrete, sensual presence chez Brenner. Melanie is unexpectedly playing the piano (Debussy's poetic 'Arabesque No. 1'), while Cathy stands nearby and indiscreetly gabs about Mitch's life. When Lydia scolds her daughter, Melanie quickly picks up a lit cigarette (she's been smoking like Hoagy Carmichael in a saloon), which is her defence mechanism around women – or birds. We learn from Cathy that Mitch spends a lot of his work time with 'hoods' in 'detention cells' (cf. the upcoming attic detention), suggesting that his interest in Melanie is partly spurred by her moral ambiguities, and that he calls San Francisco 'an anthill at the foot of a bridge', consistent with the film's Darwinian view of humanity's animality.

Cathy rattles on about a henpecking that led to murder: a client of Mitch's shot his wife six times in the head when she changed the TV channel in the middle of a ballgame. His sister confirms that Mitch, as if obeying an internal homing device, returns to his widowed mother every weekend, which resembles, as Spoto observes, Hitchcock's life with his depressed mother after his father's death at age fifty-two.[67] However, a cousin's description of Alfred's older brother William (named after his father) – 'a well-built man always smartly dressed' – sounds to me a lot more like Mitchell Brenner.[68] In fact, the license plate that Melanie spies on Mitch's Ford Galaxie – WJH 003 – bears the initials of the two William Hitchcocks (with the awkward, obese, third-born Alfred at a sibling-cancelling psychic distance?). Critics have certainly noticed Hitchcock's scatological fun with Marion's Phoenix license plate in *Psycho*: 'ANL-709'.

Cathy invites a reluctant Melanie (visibly daunted by Lydia in the kitchen) to the 'surprise' birthday party planned for the next day, details of which Cathy, as yet another female detective, has already ferreted out. Her bubbly spontaneity and increasing rapport with Melanie dramatise how staid and grandmotherly Lydia is and how bleak the house is as an environment for a growing girl. Frankly, the combined living room/dining room is poorly decorated and too harshly lit, which Hitchcock probably partly intended, but the house as seen when Melanie first steals into it uninvited is far more worked out in its furnishings and nesting spaces. The dead father's photograph – a convincingly typical, American small-town studio shot in the Rotary Club, civic-pride style – hangs like a dour Roman ancestor mask, but it's left without psychological context. Compare, in contrast, the way Hitchcock neatly supplies the missing father's complicated history around Ingrid Bergman's questionable character in *Notorious* (1946).

Most commentators on *The Birds* approve of the developing friendship between Cathy and Melanie, who softens and loses her femme fatale drive as she nurtures someone outside herself. Like most gay men and drag queens, however, I adore the bitches of Hollywood and hence do not approve at all of Melanie's enforced maturation. Like Jane Austen's Emma ('handsome, clever, and rich'), Melanie is pretentious, foolish, and to me irresistibly charming. Cathy Brenner, on the other hand, has the annoying stridency of those ever-chipper Girl Scouts and cheerleaders of 50s America; she's exactly what a nice little girl should be. I want to slap her! Cathy completely lacks the devilish moxie of Dinah, for example, Tracy Lord's hoydenish kid sister (Virginia Weidler) in *The Philadelphia Story* (1940) (who, incidentally, accompanies herself on the piano while singing a Marx Brothers tune, 'Lydia, oh, Lydia, say, have you met Lydia?'). *The Bad Seed* (1956) fiendishly parodies Cathy's type of icky-sweet, slavishly adult-pleasing, goody-goody pre-teen (Patty McCormack), who ends up a sociopathic serial murderer. That critics may have misread Hitchcock's own jaundiced view of Cathy is suggested by her resurrection in his very next film as

Jessie, a loathsomely wheedling, preening, neighbourhood princess who is pampered and spoiled by Marnie's grudging mother. My attitudes were formed early on by the gay-male irreverence of Patrick Dennis' *Auntie Mame* (1958), in which Rosalind Russell jokes about her cowering schoolboy nephew, 'If he misbehaves, we can always toss him in the river!'

Meanwhile, back in the Brenner kitchen, Mitch is helping his mother clean up. She's revealing just how much she actually knows about Melanie from the gossip columns: 'She *is* the one who jumped into a fountain in Rome last summer, isn't she? I suppose I'm old-fashioned. I know it was supposed to be very warm there, but – well, actually, the newspaper said she was naked.' Again, Tandy's delivery of Lydia's lines is superb – the quiet but slightly pushy understatement, making the risqué innuendo all the more sensational. Melanie, who later claims to have been fully clothed and pushed into the fountain, is portrayed as a rootless libertine of international café society, like the characters played by Jean Seberg in *Bonjour, Tristesse* (1958) and Anouk Aimée in Fellini's *La Dolce Vita* (1960), but here given Anita Ekberg's dunk in the Trevi Fountain. 'Darling,' Mitch firmly replies, bussing her on the cheek, 'I think I can handle Melanie Daniels by myself.'

The problem with this scene is that our first look at the private interactions of mother and son should show a bit more neuroticism or at least ambivalence on Mitch's part to do justice to the film's complex psychodynamics. Taylor is all male, with a bluff Australian heartiness that doesn't quite catch the queasy-making possibilities here. It wouldn't be fair to cite Anthony Perkins' spectacular panoply of fussy, self-deprecating mannerisms in *Psycho*, since he is playing a reclusive lunatic. But the dashing Cary Grant, as another urban careerist in *North by Northwest*, deftly captures a stymied son's sense of exasperation in his hilarious scenes with Jessie Royce Landis as his deflating mother. Suzanne Pleshette, with her savvy Jewish Freudianism, puts all the right shadings into her marvellous depiction of the articulate, hyperconscious, but slightly depressive Annie.

As Mitch bids goodbye to Melanie in her car, the driftwood on the sand behind her looks like scattered bones! – as if she is a Siren who has picked her victims clean in a Dali desert. Perhaps to regain control after his evening catering to women in the Brenner henhouse, Mitch resumes his prodding ways, suggestively teasing Melanie about her swimming adventures in Rome: 'The truth is, you were running around with a pretty wild crowd!' She gets testy under this withering cross-examination. He verbally cuffs her about and forces her to admit her lying. In his mind, he's breaking a mustang. Finally, she loses her temper and zooms off. Smugly smiling after her, Mitch suddenly notices heavy rows of crows that have been gathering on the telephone lines while Melanie was inside. He frowns, perplexed. Guess who's coming to dinner!

Back at Annie's, Melanie enters without knocking or ringing the bell – replaying her invasion of the Brenner house and treating Annie's place like a motel (cf. *Psycho*). Sitting in her bathrobe reading the women's section of the newspaper (her link, like Lydia's, to the outside world), Annie offers Melanie a brandy. It's like two military gals at the barracks, swapping tales of misadventure on the field of love. This entire scene was brilliantly conceived and designed by Hitchcock and his stellar staff, and it's phenomenally paced and executed by Hedren and Pleshette. *They* are the birds – British slang for attractive young women – as much as the film's avian marauders. Annie's sensibility is embodied in her avant-garde sculptured lamp and modernistic wall prints, seven in all, from Cubism to Modigliani. Her family could be native New Yorkers (we later hear of 'her sister in the East'), but Annie comes from bohemian San Francisco, then a centre of Beat culture. Yet she's a romantic at heart, as evidenced by the prominent album of Wagner's *Tristan and Isolde*, with its theme of self-immolation through doomed love. In Claude Chabrol's *Le Boucher* (1970), Stephane Audran's witty portrayal of the urbane, mannishly smoking, village schoolteacher is clearly an homage to Pleshette's rich, vibrant performance in *The Birds*.[69]

'Did you meet Lydia?', Annie asks, her smile showing she knows the answer. At first, Melanie doesn't want to talk about it, but soon the revelations are flowing on both sides. What we hear makes us rethink the relationship between Mitch and his mother. 'Maybe there's never been anything between Mitch and any girl,' Annie says, relating how she ended up in Bodega Bay. The more than four-year-long saga – in which her city-born relationship with Mitch went flat after her first meeting with Lydia – takes on an obsessive quality when Annie admits she moved to town just to be near him. So Annie, like Melanie, is a stalker. And like Lydia, she too lives as a forlorn widow, with her students replacing children of her own.

Wry and resigned to her self-stunted life, Annie is reluctant to blame Lydia. 'With all due respect to Oedipus,' she remarks, lifting her brandy glass in mock toast to the incest champion, Lydia is not a 'jealous woman' or a 'clinging, possessive mother' but merely fears 'being abandoned'. Most critics have accepted Annie's conclusions as those of the film itself, but I don't agree. The mother-bedevilled Hitchcock has too deliberately put devouring females at the crux of *The Birds*. And he explicitly referred to Lydia's 'unnatural relationship' to Mitch: 'She has been substituting her son for her husband.'[70] When I asked Tippi Hedren how she dealt with this in her characterisation, she said, 'I think *Melanie* thought she was a very possessive woman. It was just Annie who thought she wasn't possessive!' So Annie is in self-anaesthetising denial.

The phone rings: it's Mitch checking to make sure Melanie found her way back to Annie's. This scene is a form of sexual torture, as Annie, trapped in her own living room (and with legs drawn up, like beleaguered Melanie later on the Brenner couch), must listen to her rival accepting what are clearly Mitch's solicitous inquiries and apologies. At first 'a trifle distant' – to borrow Annie's phrase for Lydia – Melanie gradually relaxes, her reconciliation signalled by her playing with the

Melanie takes a call from Mitch at Annie's house

phone cord exactly as she did in the bird shop, but with a cigarette in hand instead of a pencil. So the film's serpentine phone cords are yet another male noose, the entrammeling by which Melanie literally twists men around her little finger.

As she heads off to bed, Melanie pulls out the Lydia-vintage flannel nightgown from her paper bag and, cocking her head like a little Dutch girl, comically poses with it for Annie. It's a form of camouflage, desexing herself to deflect Annie's jealousy after the painful phone call, which ended with Melanie agreeing to stay in town for Cathy's party tomorrow afternoon, where Annie expected to have Mitch to herself. Suddenly there's a noise at the door: thinking it's a knock, Annie again calls out, 'Who is it?' She opens the door to find a dead gull at the threshold. So Melanie's missing knock has been supplied by the hurtling bird, her proxy. 'Poor thing,' Annie says, 'Probably lost his way in the dark.' She pities it and, as always, assumes the best. Melanie of battered brow suspects something more: 'But it isn't dark, Annie. There's a full moon.' The women turn and stare at each other with frozen, white, mirrored profiles as a ghostly blue landscape opens behind them. This is one of the most genuinely eerie moments in the film. We have reverted to paganism, when the movements of birds were omens and when the sun, moon and stars exerted occult influence on human life.

Daylight again: Melanie and Mitch, carrying martini glasses, are climbing a high, windy dune overlooking the salt flat of the bay at low tide (no exit by sea!). They remind me of dyspeptic partygoers Jeanne Moreau and Marcello Mastroianni wandering out on a golf course at dawn in Antonioni's *La notte* (1960). We see the distant town and mountains and, far below, the birthday party in full swing on the sunny Brenner lawn. Amid the birdlike cries of the children rises Annie's organising voice. She is the governess in love with the lord who mates within his own class; hence she is condemned to melancholy voyeurism. 'Atta girl, come on, don't let him get you!', Annie calls out to a child, but Melanie, trailed by Mitch, turns her head, since it subliminally echoes the boat scene and applies to her here too.

The dune discourse is perhaps the worst photographed scene in the film; it's too blatantly done in the studio, with bad lighting and sound. And there is some controversy about the dialogue: scriptwriter Evan Hunter did not write this scene and even acidly speculated that Tippi Hedren 'ad libbed her way through it'.[71] But Hedren categorically denies

The disintegrating titles; Melanie at Union Square and driving to Bodega Bay

Downtown Bodega Bay; Melanie returning to town and then struck by the gull

First aid at the diner; Annie and Melanie find a dead gull; martinis
at the birthday party

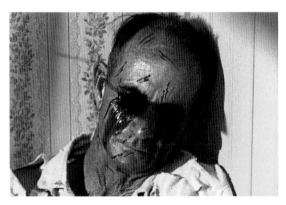

Dan Fawcett's corpse

Melanie crossing the bay; Lydia's truck speeding home; Melanie at
the jungle gym

53

Before the attack; Melanie, Mrs Bundy, and Sebastian; the town in chaos

Melanie in the telephone booth; Bodega Bay burns; attack night at
the Brenners

Melanie collapses in the attic; hope for escape; last shot of the film

this. Melanie surveys her life: on Mondays and Wednesdays working for 'the Traveller's Aid at the airport' (doing migration studies, presumably); on Tuesdays taking 'a course in general semantics at Berkeley' (another cackling bird shop); and on Thursdays having fund-raising lunch-meetings for 'sending a little Korean boy through school'. The effect is campy and decadent. Melanie has been designer-grazing through life with what Spoto aptly calls 'social and intellectual dilettantism', the anomie of those who inherit money rather than earning it for themselves.[72] For me, the highlight of this scene is the exquisite grace with which Hedren, with her lacquered red nails, holds and sips from the crystalline martini glass: this too is civilisation!

When Melanie boasts of her plan to scandalise her 'prim' aunt with the trash-talking mynah, Mitch jokes, 'You need a mother's care, my child.' Perhaps irked by his condescension, she sharply changes mood: 'My mother? Don't waste your time! [Cf. gardener Annie: 'There's a lot of time in Bodega Bay.'] She ditched us when I was eleven and ran off with some hotel man in the East.' So Melanie, in displacing Lydia, also risks falling backward into eleven-year-old Cathy. The abandoned daughter who avoids hotels has a mother who behaves like a philandering man – or an escaped bird. 'I don't know where she is,' Melanie murmurs, her voice breaking as her brittle persona starts to crack. 'Well, maybe I ought to go join the other children,' she ruefully remarks, recovering her humour but acknowledging her loss of control.

As the two start down the slope, the children are shown playing blindman's buff, which stands for the social game of love, in which friend and foe are often the same. United in common anguish, Annie and Lydia stare paralysed at Melanie and Mitch descending as a couple. Just before the latter reach ground level, gulls unleash the film's first mass attack. Is their wrath an externalisation of the buried animosities and murderous jealousies of the triangulated women? – just as the inner chaos of Dr Morbius becomes an invisible monster in *Forbidden Planet* (1956).

Blindfolded Cathy is the first hit – at which point I usually cheer. 'Hey, no touching allowed!', she yelps as her head is slammed (like Melanie's in the boat), which sounds a lot like Lydia's puritanical maxim for her children. The little party with its tidy table of white cake and pink punch – the kind of sanitised entertainment paternalistic adults have always thought proper for young people – is rudely cancelled by the ravening birds, much as Phineus' banquet was befouled by flying female Harpies.[73] As if playing a carnival game, the gulls dive for the balloons, which hang like mammary and phallic fruits from the arbour: pop! go human illusions. The motif of blindman's buff at a children's party occurs in *Young and Innocent*, which opens with a female corpse floating like seaweed near gull-covered rocks. And in *Strangers on a Train*, the cynical murderer pops a boy's balloon with his burning cigarette at the amusement park, where the whirling carousel, with its plunging, ornamented animals, is another symbol for the social dance.

My favourite detail in *The Birds*' party scene is the little girl in patent-leather shoes lying face down on the grass and kicking her legs like a windmill, as her sky-blue dress and crinoline slip hike up and a gull steadily pecks the back of her head. 'Ow, ow, ow!', she and it seem to cry in tandem. It's like that famous definition of Surrealism: 'the chance encounter of an umbrella and a sewing machine on a dissecting table'. Melanie, now the agile rescuer, whips off her fine jacket to lash the gull away. Hitchcock's masterful cutting of this helter-skelter episode makes us feel the blind panic of the group as they scatter and run about in every direction like – well, chickens with their heads cut off. Annie athletically fells the addled Cathy with a super flying tackle, and the adults drag and carry the children into the house to take cover, like fugitives from strafing warplanes. 'That makes three times,' pronounces Annie like a Roman augur to Melanie. The scene ends with two little girls' frightened faces peering up at the sky – a redhead holding a party napkin to her scratched cheek (the only injury Hitchcock allows the children) and the brunette saved by Melanie.

After all the guests are gone except Melanie, the stunned Brenners sit down in the living room for a simple meal of leftover roast-beef sandwiches with coffee. The house seems as bunkered as their mood. Peevishly covering the cage of the agitated lovebirds with a white table napkin, Lydia tries to hurry Melanie off and, with something of Mrs Danvers' animus as implacable guardian-of-the-house in *Rebecca*, even wheels around her with flashing table knife erect. But Cathy and Mitch want Melanie to stay. As they bicker, there's an intimate, angled close-up of Melanie's stricken, almost telepathic face as she alone hears a warning crescendo of cheeps and notices a sparrow on the hearth. With a roar, thousands of birds descending through the chimney explode from the fireplace, spraying a cloud of choking grey ash over everyone's food.

Birds explode from the chimney

Birds divebombing Lydia

Has the female turf war created a moral vacuum that sucks the flock down the flue? 'Cover your faces! Cover your eyes!', shouts Mitch, defending the basic terms of human identity amid the crazy din of flapping and chirping. It's like a closed circle of Dante's Inferno, with the damned tossed about in a vortex of erratic winds and filthy air. Hitchcock, the Grand Inquisitor, has flipped compulsions, tormenting his cast in the prior scene by agoraphobia and in this one by claustrophobia.

We never seem to see food passing anyone's lips inside the Brenner home. Mitch pulls the napkin off the cage to flail at the swarming birds and upends the food-laden table to block the chimney. Tangled birds are disassembling Lydia's hairdo as she hysterically staggers near the massive mantel clock (driving her cuckoo?), while Cathy buries her head in the newly maternal Melanie's lap. Melanie has the presence of mind to grab Lydia's arm, and the women escape through the French doors, abandoning the house to the birds. Next we see deputy sheriff Al Malone surveying the wreckage of the room and denying, in the usual way of slow-witted cops of science-fiction films, that there's any reason to worry. The numbed Lydia wanders about straightening pictures and picking up broken teacups – which Wood calls a 'leitmotif' in the film

Lydia picks through her ruins (frame enlargement)

symbolising human 'fragility' – while Melanie silently watches, feeling compassion for Lydia for the first time but also realising that the power balance has shifted.[74] Hitchcock said that Lydia's behaviour shows she is literally 'cracking up'.[75] 'I'll take Cathy up to bed,' Melanie announces, deciding to stay the night. As she and Cathy chummily depart with arms entwined around waists, Lydia stares at them blankly – the second time today she's had to face Melanie's insinuating couplings. Melanie the cuckoo has moved in and usurped the mother's role.

Cut to early next morning: in a beautifully composed shot, Mitch is raking a smoky fire at lawn's edge, with the bay and mountains behind him. This mysterious activity was explained by Hitchcock to Truffaut: an entire scene has been cut in which Mitch, burning the dead birds in a bonfire, chats tensely with Melanie, who comes outside with her fur coat piquantly thrown over her nightgown.[76] What we do see, as usual, is Melanie at a mirror: her soft hair fetchingly down, she is applying lipstick in the tiny, old-fashioned room where she has spent the night. She hears Lydia's voice calling out that she's going to drop Cathy off (plainly at school) and then drive over to the Fawcett farm. From the second-story window, Melanie sees Lydia's turquoise truck pulling away – in the original script providing a golden opportunity for a tête-à-tête with Mitch.

We stay with the truck for one of the most famous and admired episodes in Hitchcock's work. Lydia streaks across the broad green meadows of the Fawcett property, combining the images of Melanie's sports car traversing the countryside with that of her boat bisecting the bay. Both women seem to carve the screen's horizontals by sheer, blunt will-power. Lydia's truck makes the same, gravelly sweep of the Fawcett barnyard that Melanie's car did at the Brenners'. Exchanging quick greetings with the hired hand, who hasn't seen Dan Fawcett yet this morning, Lydia marches up the walk and knocks. When there's no answer, she opens the door and goes straight in, just as Melanie did on her first mission.

As Lydia moves hesitantly through the kitchen, we spot an elk's head mounted in the next room, implying that the Fawcett tastes are more rugged than those of the Brenner house, where the father's image presides over a spinet piano adorned with pastoral rococo porcelain figurines. As she pauses by a row of shattered teacups still hanging on their hooks, the camera zooms in slightly to mark her inner shock, registered on her face only by her widening eyes. Again, we see a female detective, putting two and two together. The broken teacups, recalling the title sequence of broken letters, are signs of a woman's past presence in the house: if Dan Fawcett is a widower, might Lydia have been considering remarriage? – in which case her reconnoitring even more resembles Melanie's, with the ruined teacups representing her dashed hopes.

Purse dangling from her arm, Lydia slowly walks down a long, unlit, grey hall (like Melanie's linear track on the dock) and uneasily half-enters a room strewn with silent evidence of a frenzy of Delacroix-like destruction – pictures askew, bibelots shattered, and a dead gull grotesquely caught in the smashed window. Hitchcock's cuts follow her eye movements, as she notices more and more – the shredded windowshade (cf. *Psycho*'s slotted hotel blinds and ripped shower curtain), tipped lamp, scattered feathers, tossed books, a dung-soiled shoe, and a dead crow on the bed. It's like the surreal trail of objects – oranges, magazine, wooden spoon, playing cards, checkerboard – that leads to a corpse and then Constance Porter at the start of *Lifeboat*. Glancing down, Lydia sees on the floor, cut by the edge of the open door,

A horrified Lydia flees the Fawcett farmhouse

a man's bare, bloody feet and ripped pyjama legs. As she takes another step, three, quick, closer and closer cuts reveal the farmer propped up in the corner: we are literally pulled into his face, where crimson gore has poured from his pecked-out eyes.

There has been an oppressive hush throughout this scene, broken now only by Lydia careening back down the hall, her arms desperately raised (like Melanie's in the attic) and her purse dropping with a thud. Next, she is seen hurtling directly toward us down the front walk (another linear path), with the wild, half-crouching movements not of a dignified matron but of a terrified child or scrambling animal. Eyes half-deranged and mouth gaping, she is utterly mute, the syllables strangled in her gurgling throat. Pushing past the bewildered farmhand, she leaps in her truck and roars off, hunched over the steering wheel as if it were a life-preserver. Hitchcock described how he 'made the truck carry on for her': 'the screech of the truck engine starting off conveys her anguish'; 'it's as though the truck were shrieking', expressed also by the 'whizzing' and the 'cloud of dust', with smoke added to the truck's exhaust. For Lydia's slower approach to the Fawcett farm, Hitchcock said, 'I had the road watered down'.[77]

As the speeding truck veers into the Brenner drive, it looks as if Lydia is hellbent to cut down Mitch and Melanie, who are embracing (or rather billing and cooing like lovebirds, with Melanie indecorously still in nightgown and slippers) near the rail fence, framed by the cage-like gazebo. The missing scene had showed the two arguing, then coming together in shared anxiety over the bird attack. When they rush to Lydia's aid as she half-tumbles from the truck, she violently shoves them apart (her secret wish), moaning with misanthropic disgust, before running sobbing into the house.

Hitchcock said he had got 'the idea for the gouged-out eyes of the dead man' from a true story told him by a Bodega farmer about crows killing his lambs.[78] But the motif occurs decades earlier in *Young and Innocent* in a cheeky boy's lunchtime fantasy of a fugitive dying of hunger in the field 'with rooks pecking at his eyes'. Furthermore, with self-blinded Oedipus already in the script, thanks to Annie, it's possible to see Lydia traumatised not just by the external atrocity but by her recognition of her own inner, castrating demons. Dan, the fallen father figure, looks like a rape victim, like Annie later. Asked by Bogdanovich how he would define 'pure cinema', Hitchcock gave the example of

Lydia's glimpses of Dan's eyes: 'The staccato jumps are about catching the breath. Gasp. Gasp. Yes.'[79] Elsewhere, Hitchcock said not using the expected zoom here also allowed him 'to be prepared for censorship problems'.[80]

It's like a mathematical diagram of the process of perception: Lydia looks by stages, taking in data, with the conclusion of the syllogism the awful zeroes of the farmer's eyes. We saw those same inky sockets in the grinning skull of Mrs Bates, as her mummy swings around toward us in the fruit cellar of *Psycho*. Wood usefully compares Lydia's experience to Mrs Moore's in the Marabar cave in E.M. Forster's *A Passage to India*: there is nothing to say because both women have confronted the ultimate chaos of existence, beyond space and time, reason and language, love and hate.[81] Howard Smit did the amazing make-up on the dead farmer (played by a stuntman), whose eyes were covered with 'dumold, an undertaker's wax' and then 'heavily blackened'.[82] In retrospect, these images have gained prophetic power about the 60s: Hitchcock seems to have anticipated that decade's thrill killings and political assassinations, with their fatal head wounds, as well as the senseless looting and riots. And the Dionysian excesses of psychedelia too: Dan Fawcett's dead eyes, with their tracks of bloody tears, look like those of the drugged Beatles staring into the void in Richard Avedon's classic Day-Glo icons for *Life* magazine.

Later that morning, Melanie is exchanging sweet nothings with Mitch in the kitchen, while she prepares tea for Lydia, an invalid upstairs. Now lady of the house, Melanie has dressed and put her hair up but has deferentially left off her earrings and opulent gold-braid necklace, never to return in the film. Seeing crockery in one piece on the tray seems to restore Lydia as much as the tea itself, as if Humpty Dumpty can be put back together again. Her bedroom's ormolu clock, London city prints, and heavy gilt mirror suggest that Lydia or her parents were not natively Californian or even American: she too may be a migrant. Lydia is at her most confessional, and Melanie, glancing at the baby pictures on the mantelpiece, is genuinely moved by Lydia's admission of her fears and lack of her late husband's natural rapport with children. Hitchcock slows the pace, recovering the rhythms of daily life, as a lull between storms. When Lydia obsessively harps on the vulnerability of the big schoolhouse windows ('All the windows are broken in Dan's bedroom'), Melanie offers to go and pick up Cathy, once again taking on the mother's role. The women have achieved a wary truce, signalled by Lydia thanking Melanie by her first name.

Pulling up to the schoolhouse, Melanie hears the children inside being led by Annie in a round song, whose monotonous, floating lines describe a character like Tennyson's Mariana or the Lady of Shalott, a woman in perpetual mourning like both Lydia and Annie: 'She combed her hair but once a year, / With every stroke she shed a tear.' Perhaps it's Melanie too, whose tightly wound hair expresses her armoured personality, forged by her mother's neglect. Signalled by Annie (who wears a pendant watch on a gold steward's chain – time hangs heavily for her in Bodega Bay) to wait until the peculiar lesson ends, Melanie wanders toward the playground and sits down on a bench, with the jungle gym behind her.

Taking a cigarette from a chic, enamelled black box in her purse (cf. Annie's more available-for-pleasure, mashed pack), Melanie proceeds to smoke her way through her hiatus, in a combination of boredom, impatience and anxiety. She turns repeatedly to look over her left shoulder at the schoolhouse, where the children are sounding like a broken record (a comment by Hitchcock on his adolescent curriculum-by-catechism?). She is literally marking time. Meanwhile, over her right shoulder, seen only by the audience, crow after crow is landing on the jungle gym, by exponential incrementation. The ninety-second scene is drawn out to excruciating length: clock time, under emotional duress, is pulled and stretched like a melting watch by Dali. Hitchcock told his art director that the oblivious Melanie's final close-up should be held 'until the audience can't stand it'.[83]

This is another of Tippi Hedren's great scenes. Hitchcock's masterful cuts, which have been studied by film-makers worldwide, have unfortunately overshadowed what Hedren accomplishes here, with her crisp, elegant body language and rapid, fluid facial expressions. Like Lydia's tour of the Fawcett farmhouse, it's done entirely in mime. Stylishly tapping and flicking her cigarette as her eyes rove in sync with her unsettled thoughts, Hedren's Melanie makes us contemplate female mannerisms from an anthropological distance. Or should one say ornithological: Melanie seems as if she belongs in the 'delicate' little Chinese paintings of birds that Hitchcock originally planned to use for the titles.[84]

Hedren's formal, economical movements in this scene have so bewitched me over the years that I asked her if in fact she was a smoker at the time. 'Yes, I was,' she replied. 'I started smoking because when I was modelling, I was sent out to go see the people about a Chesterfield commercial for a Perry Como Show, and I didn't smoke. And they said, "Well, you *have* to smoke." So I *learned* how to smoke just for that.' In other words, Hedren from the start conceived of smoking as a *visual activity*: this would eventually produce her disciplined gestures in *The Birds*, where she demonstrates what a friend of mine calls 'the fine art of smoking'. Hedren acknowledged that her professional background was probably formative of her on-screen body language: 'I started modelling when I was thirteen, and I think that gives you a great sense of posture.'

The enormous burden of crows on the jungle gym, when Melanie finally sees them, is almost like an accumulation of her fears and fantasies – to which she reacts with the same horror as Lydia looking into the farmer's obliterated eyes. The iron frame itself resembles the unfurling Bauhaus grid of Saul Bass' great title sequence for *North by Northwest*. It represents social structure and, in *The Birds*, fate or Necessity. The jungle gym is where children clamber like monkeys as they practise for adulthood – learning the ropes, as it were, on the webbed rigging of life's voyage. Over the years, Hitchcock's jungle gym came to symbolise civilisation itself for me, and it influenced my theory of Apollonian form in *Sexual Personae*. Hitchcock's vision of architecture as the grand but eternally provisional frame of human meaning is evident everywhere in his major films, from the glass-skinned towers of *North by Northwest* and the arched suspension bridge of *Vertigo* to the cantilevered brassieres designed by Barbara Bel Geddes in the same film.[85]

When Melanie, following a lone crow arcing over her, sees the massed birds, she bolts up and backs away. The loaded jungle gym seems like a single monstrous being, a mammoth skeleton rippling with mouldering flesh from the grave. It's like a combination of Baudelaire's poems, 'Carrion', where seething maggots devour a carcass in a sunny park, and 'Voyage to Cythera', where the poet, castrated by carnivorous birds, hangs crucified on his own guilt-ridden body. Indeed, Hitchcock's jungle gym could be called *Labyrinth of the Guilt Complex* – the book that psychoanalyst Ingrid Bergman studies in *Spellbound* (1945). The camera, tracking through Melanie's eyes as she edges toward the schoolhouse, seems to glide like her boat on the bay. It's as if her overloaded brain is in suspended animation and no longer controls her legs or feet.

Melanie catches Annie just as she flings open the side door to send the children out to recess. The teacher then devises a deceptive strategy that doesn't seem very smart: announcing a fire drill (more prescient than she knows), at which the surprised children screech like birds, she sends them into the street to go home or to the hotel – that mysterious establishment shunned by Melanie. The birds aren't fooled one bit. As soon as the little snacks hit the road, the crows rise from the gym (fifteen feet of film had to be edited out 'when a couple of eager birds missed their cue and flew off ahead of the others') and, in a process shot, soar up from behind the schoolhouse like a cloud of bats.[86] Academe breeds nightmares.

It's another race, this time foot versus wing. Like Furies, the crows harass the children from behind, nipping their necks and cheeks, as we seem to slide helplessly backward downhill, with the mob about to trample us. There's a tremendous noise of mingled screams and raucous bird cries. After the first flash of real horror, I generally settle down to laughing and applauding the crows, whom I regard as Coleridgean emissaries vandalising sentimental Wordsworthian notions of childhood. It's like my idol Keith Richards cuffing about Pollyanna and Beaver Cleaver. There's an exuberant, Saturnalian, *Mad* magazine zaniness to the whole grisly business. Hitchcock's victims will graduate to sadists in a scene in Roger Vadim's *Barbarella* (1968), clearly influenced by this one, where Jane Fonda is attacked by an advancing battalion of fanged dolls who take bloody nips out of her legs and chain mail.

Swept along, but of course never without her purse, Melanie can only run with the pack like a troop leader on forced retreat at Pamplona. When one child falls flat, shattering her glasses (a motif from Eisenstein's *Potemkin* that Hitchcock also used in *Strangers on a Train*), Cathy and Melanie rush back to help, and then the three take shelter in a station wagon, hit on every side by birds.[87] It's like the later scene in the telephone booth, but here the glass holds. When Melanie tries to start the car, the key is missing (cf. the peekaboo key of *Notorious*), which suggests her inability to make sense of what's happening. Immobilised for the first time in a car, she honks the squawking horn in frustration, then rests her head in exhaustion on the steering wheel, as the bird attack peters off. (I'm always vexed here, muttering, 'For heaven's sake, put the car in neutral, and roll down the hill!') The horizon-line speedometer is stuck at zero: Melanie the daring driver has become a pedestrian, as

Melanie and the schoolchildren pursued by the crows (studio shot)

The schoolchildren in flight along the Bodega road (location shot)

desperate with her two charges on the open road as Sophia Loren as a war refugee with a gang-raped daughter in *Two Women* (1961).

Next we see Melanie, hair mussed but composure restored, speaking to 'Daddy' by long distance on the house phone at the restaurant bar. We don't miss Cathy (who would?), but Melanie must have taken her back up the hill to Annie's house – which, as it will turn out, puts her in far more danger. After the tacky frenzy of the crow chase, it's a pleasure to watch Melanie in sophisticated top form again. Hedren's cultivated, melodious voice (another distinctive feature for which she's been underappreciated) sounds even lovelier than usual after the bird cacophony. As always when talking to men, Melanie thoughtfully massages the curlicue phone cord. Briefing her newpaperman father on the attacks, she manages to alarm the packed lunchtime crowd. Hitchcock has prankishly seated her under a sign, 'Absolutely No Credit', which seems to allude not only to her worry-free affluence but to her history of lying: she who has cried minx so often will soon not be believed. Another sign, for cheap, proletarian 'Gallo Wine' (Hitchcock was a snobbish oenophile), flags the nearness of the Sonoma and Napa Valley vineyards.

The great restaurant episode, which Truffaut initially felt was 'too long', is like a play within a play.[88] As I see it, the first act, seamlessly woven by Evan Hunter, consists of nine tense minutes of collective dialogue before the attacks resume; the second act is the tornado of destruction in the town square, and the third is Melanie's ostracism by a pitiless female jury. The tripartite sequence, totaling fourteen minutes, demonstrates the full range of Hitchcock's genius, from his shrewd notation of everyday behaviour and his seductive manipulation of emotion to his acrobatic staging of action scenes. What I find especially superb is the nearly Cubist series of establishing shots of the restaurant interior, with Melanie the pivot point: we are shown every door, wall, person and potted plant from different angles. Space is like an opaque medium that Hitchcock knows how to carve, trim and slice as if it were a side of beef. Each character here is minutely individuated by dress, manner and speech. The diner is like a zoo, or rather Noah's ark, with everyone jammed in like the bobbing, bantering survivors of *Lifeboat*.

As Melanie talks on the phone, the formidable Mrs Bundy arrives to buy cigarettes. Played by Ethel Griffies, an 84-year-old veteran British actress whom Hitchcock knew from his London years, she is a walking embodiment of the kind of forceful personalities of the first wave of post-suffrage feminism whom I revere. With her rakish French beret, Norfolk stalking jacket, and stentorian, oratorical voice, she radiates arrogant self-confidence and a no-nonsense, can-do attitude toward life. The third of the complex women whom Melanie confronts and comes to respect, she is a learned amateur ornithologist who supplies the scientific lore of the film. Hitchcock gets wonderful humour from the way Melanie's annoyance at being contradicted and upstaged by Mrs Bundy gradually turns into charmed fascination. The crusty old lady, stop-and-start lighting her thick cigarette with paper matches, is the only person in the film except the children who is blithely indifferent to Melanie's sexual charisma. Mrs Bundy is beyond vanity, as is shown by her not bothering to look at herself in the cigarette-machine mirror.[89]

Hedren told me: 'I *loved* watching Ethel Griffies! She was just *amazing*, totally amazing. That thing with the cigarette was her idea – the way she holds the cigarette, and everyone's thinking, "Oh, God, she's going to burn her fingers!"' When I said that the large cast in the taut restaurant scene seemed to work as smoothly as an ensemble, Hedren agreed: 'It's from getting to know everybody in a six-month shoot, which was a long period of time. You get to know everyone very well and become a family.' She spoke of how 'totally exhausting' this 'ordeal' got: 'Because I was in the every frame, I had one afternoon off in the entire six months – and then I had to go to the dentist!' In other words, the cast was really living *The Birds* as it was made, an intensity that truly shows in the final result. An analogy might be David Lean's long production of *Lawrence of Arabia* (1962), where for five months in Jordan the cast suffered the same excruciating desert conditions as the characters they played.

'Sam, three Southern fried chicken!', barks the waitress, breaking into Mrs Bundy's Wordsworthian disquisition on the gentle, non-aggressive nature of birds. The script's comic polyphony interweaves cerebral speculation with the coarse, common world of material appetite. The eaters and the eaten switch roles: it's humans, not birds, who will end up on the menu. As Mrs Bundy waxes eloquent about the lyrical beauty of our feathered friends, a dithery mother fusses over her two children: in a stew over the jawing about bird attacks, she overprotects her interested but not particularly upset chicks to the point of neurosis, much as Henry James' manic governess in *The Turn of the Screw* terrorises her charge into a heart attack.

The argument about the moral nature of birds breaks into a full-scale philosophical symposium, accompanied by food and drink in the Greek manner. An unshaven overimbiber with a heavy Irish brogue (an O'Casey character, according to Hitchcock, who filmed *Juno and the Paycock*, with its loquacious layabouts, in 1930) cites the Bible: 'It's the end of the world!' This Providential view of the birds as agents of wrathful supernatural power is satirised, but it dovetails with Mrs Bundy's fantasies of Christian compassion (she catalogues area birds in 'our Christmas count'). And it's seconded in a different way by the brusque cannery owner (eating with un-Brenner-like gusto), who growls that gulls 'have been playing devil with my fishing boats' and, nearly capsizing one boat, 'practically tore the skipper's arm off'. Insisting that the birds tried to kill the children, Melanie allows for the kind of motiveless murder near and dear to the director of *Rope*, which was inspired by the real-life Leopold and Loeb case.

Despite her tender feeling for birds, the crushing statistics that Mrs Bundy pedantically unleashes provide the scene's climax: 'Birds have been on this planet, Miss Daniels, since archaeopteryx – 140 million years ago.' There are '8,650 species of birds' and '100 billion birds' in the world today; should all these species band together, 'we wouldn't have a chance!' As if in illustration, the true story of the Santa Cruz seagull invasion is recounted by a travelling salesman and confirmed by Mrs Bundy, with details drawn directly from the 1961 *Sentinel* newspaper article. 'Poor things,' she says of the dead birds, just like Annie at the full moon. Another of the waitress' loud interjections – 'Two Bloody Marys, Deke!' – capsulises the scene's real theme of Mother Nature red in tooth and claw.

As the hysterical mother foolishly goads the tipsy, foul-mouthed salesman to guide her to the escape route to San Francisco, the newly arrived Mitch confers *sotto voce* with the seaman, Sebastian, and proposes an emergency strategy to save the town by mimicking the Santa Cruz fog with army smoke bombs ("Make our own fog!' – a wry comment by the script on the human hunger for meaning?). As if fatigued with all this guy talk, Melanie drifts toward the window and hears a bird cry before anyone else does: that this may again be telepathy is suggested by the odd clarity of the noise through what will prove to be heavy, sound-muffling plate glass. As at the jungle gym, her eyes follow the off-camera arcing trajectory of invasion.

The next chain of incidents, interlocked and escalating, is so operatically designed and edited that it's like a Baroque *danse macabre*. A glancing blow by a swooping gull, as in Melanie's attack, sets it all into motion, like Yeats' swan falling on Leda, which triggers the massacres and conflagrations of ancient history. There's a violent series of solo performances, all abrupt pirouettes and falls. A stricken mechanic pumping gas sprawls and rolls backwards, dropping the gushing hose, from which a toxic stream zigzags directly toward us. The salesman, confused by the gabble of onlookers squawking a warning, drops the match from his cigar and swivels, cooked to a crisp, in a pillar of fire. Melanie, trapped in the 'cage of misery' of the telephone booth (like Marion Crane's shower), spins and struggles like a genie in a bottle, filmed from above as she turns and turns in the town's widening gyre.[90] An unlucky passerby, face gored, who staggers to the booth like a ghoulish suitor wanting to dance, stares at Melanie with the shocked, unseeing eyes of *Psycho*'s Arbogast, falling backwards with knifed face down the mansion stairs. Even the snaky fire hose, spraying a massive cone of water against the jolted phone booth, seems to dance to its own mad music.

72   The gas station explodes (frame enlargement)

As the occupants of the diner cluster at the window, there are four, cartoon-like stills of Melanie's frozen face, mouth open in prophetic horror, as she watches the rush of fire back along the gasoline trail to explode the tanks in a great mushroom cloud, incinerating the town centre. While the famous bird's eye view shows, as I have noted earlier, a fire specially set in the studio parking lot, a real car was actually blown up on location in Bodega Bay to assure the realism of Hedren's responses. Melanie's 'ordeal by fire', as Hitchcock put it, also turned out to be Hedren's.[91] Despite a protective pane of glass, she told me, her eyeballs were burned and remained 'flaming bright red' for several days, requiring medicated eyedrops: 'It was terrible!' Furthermore, when the fake bird hit the phone booth's supposedly shatterproof panel, Hedren says, 'it still broke into my face', and tiny pieces of glass flew into her cheeks: 'You see my reaction.' The shards had to be removed at the studio clinic. The giant spiderweb pattern made by that blow is one of the film's recurrent motifs. Alternately symbolising female sexuality and nature's brutality, it appears in the schoolchild's broken eyeglasses; the vent window of Lydia's truck as she flees the Fawcett farm; and the rear window of yet another turquoise truck near the immolated salesman. All three have seen too much.

The aerial shot (suddenly quiet, with a crescendo of interoffice bird chat) shows a jagged line of fire that looks like a rune or a message to the Peruvian sky-gods scored in the desert plateau at Nazca. A superb example of what Hitchcock, in another context, called 'the free abstract in moviemaking', it reminds me of the triangle (the 'Avenger's' calling card) that is superimposed on a London map in *The Lodger*. Hitchcock told Truffaut that he did the 'high shot' of *The Birds* 'to show the exact topography of Bodega Bay'.[92] As a child, Hitchcock loved maps and memorised timetables, the Apollonian lore of life reconceived as geometry and number. From the air, the scavenging birds gaze impersonally at Bodega Bay, turning human home, schoolhouse and civic plaza into their very own grocery stores.

As civilisation collapses in Bodega Bay – with the police and fire companies helpless and an incongruous, horse-drawn wagon stampeding out of the wild West (or Hitchcock père's Covent Garden) to strew cabbages in the street – Mitch pulls the tearful Melanie from the booth and into the sanctuary of the restaurant. Relief immediately turns to apprehension at the eerie silence – usually a prelude to discovering corpses in this film. What they find around a corner is just as still and almost as chilling: a row of women diners and waitresses, huddled like survivors of a blitz or shipwreck. After the punishing gauntlet Melanie has run, from the schoolhouse onwards, with objects whirling at her from every direction, the last thing she expects or deserves is this sudden, terrible isolation, where she seems to stand naked before the tribunal of the outraged community. She has become the ritual scapegoat, as in Shirley Jackson's 'The Lottery'.

The shrill mother, like a witch-baiter in *The Crucible*, advances on Melanie, whose point of view is taken by the camera and therefore us: 'They said when you got here, the whole thing started. Who are you? What are you? Where did you come from? I think you're the cause of all this. I think you're evil – *evil*!' Melanie, having had quite enough of impossible mothers, smacks her solidly in the face – which breaks the spell, but there is still no movement to Melanie's side. While the woman's charges are too irrational and sensational to accept in naturalistic terms, they have a mythic power that cannot be shaken off: on some level, Melanie really is a kind of vampire attuned to nature's occult messages.

Hand in hand, Mitch and Melanie now flee up the deserted road, as if they were Adam and Eve expelled from the Garden by a hell's angel with flaming tongue. Hitchcock himself acerbically cited the post-nuclear *On the Beach* (1959) as a narratively weaker parallel to *The Birds*: this scene in particular recalls Gregory Peck and Ava Gardner bleakly awaiting the final chapter in global destruction.[93] The only living things are crows lined up (resting after lunch?) on the schoolhouse roof and jungle gym. As Mitch and Melanie approach Annie's house beyond the playground, the camera smoothly tracks, in the ominous Hitchcock way, past the white picket fence, lateral peepholes through which we strain to see. Annie's lifeless body appears like a dropped doll or fallen mannequin, her legs twisted up on the steps. The bloody gashes on her bare limbs make her look like a victim of rape-murder. The image combines Lydia's race down the Fawcett walk with the corpse she flees, but this is worse: a human body left exposed to the elements has been ethically unbearable since long before Sophocles' *Antigone*. Mitch keeps Melanie out – corpse inspection is man's work – and us too, as he shades Annie's presumably pecked-out eyes with his cupped hand (cf. his cupped hand in the bird shop). A morbid detail is the fly that Hitchcock

Hitchcock directs Annie's death scene

Mitch hides Annie's bloody eyes, as Melanie retches

has somehow managed to capture crawling on Annie's leg ('I'm not even going to swat that fly,' says Norman-as-Mother at the end of *Psycho*).

'Cathy! Where's Cathy?', Melanie screeches, hunched over as if to vomit, her voice high and childlike. Shellshocked from her traumas and perhaps touched by Freudian guilt over her rival's extermination (which simplifies the erotic triangle), she has begun to regress – a slide that will continue until film's end. She merges with Cathy, who is seen, hale and hearty, grimacing tearfully from the curtained window. I sigh crossly here, more than willing to sacrifice little Iphigenia Brenner to give Suzanne Pleshette some more scenes. Melanie must stop the enraged Mitch from throwing a stone at the birds: we have literally returned to the Stone Age, after technological man's machines have failed and science has proved inadequate for understanding nature's cruel mysteries. When Mitch gravely covers the body with his jacket, he and we reflect on his implication in this tragedy, for he brought Annie to Bodega Bay.

As Melanie and the trembling Cathy desperately embrace, Mitch must jog Melanie's arm to hand her her purse. A sign of her degeneration (or radical remaking) is that this is the second scene in a row where Melanie has forgotten her purse! – the waitress had to run after her with it as Melanie and Mitch retreated from the diner. Haggling, shrewd-shopper Lydia also abandoned her precious purse in extremity. The none-too-solid canvas top (another cage cover) now goes up for the first time on Melanie's convertible. We learn from sobbing Cathy in the car that Annie and she had stepped onto the porch when they heard the explosion downtown: 'All at once, the birds were everywhere!' Shoving Cathy inside, Annie was cut down – another victim of careless smoking. Hitchcock was kinder: 'She sacrificed herself to protect the sister of the man she loves. It's her final gesture.'[94]

The transition to the long, last section of the film is the sound of hammering, prelude to a crucifixion. The camera pans the facade of the shuttered Brenner house, whose windows have been unevenly boarded up with jagged, weathered planks. Architecture is devolving: Mitch has evidently torn apart a barn to turn the house into a blind bunker. It's back to cave-man days. High on a ladder, Mitch in his green-khaki safari pants is nailing up the attic windows, while Melanie, as if carrying her own cross, hands up a big piece of timber: she has a predestined appointment on that very floor.[95] Mitch as prudent householder is preparing for an avian missile crisis: when *The Birds* was made,

Annie Hayworth may be dead, but Suzanne Pleshette lives! (location shot at Bodega Bay)

Americans were just emerging from the Cold War in which bomb shelters, or at least ample emergency provisions of food and water (with which my father stocked our cellar), were advised for private homes. The couple glance uneasily at Bodega Bay: birds rise from the marsh, while black smoke hangs over the distant town, as if it were Berlin or Sodom. Have the birds taken vengeance for Mitch's bonfire holocaust?

'The phone's dead,' Melanie says, for the first time unable to reach her all-protecting father. So it's the end of the line for the phone theme, whose climax was Melanie's entrapment with a pay phone that she was too frantic and purseless to use. Lydia summons them to listen to San Francisco news on the radio, their last link with the outside world (a du Maurier detail), which is reporting the problems in Bodega Bay: a 'seriously injured' girl – presumably the one with lacerated face whom Melanie pulled into the station wagon – has been taken to the hospital in Santa Rosa. Explicitly worried about the attic windows, Lydia wants to leave, but Mitch thinks it's unsafe. At this point Lydia goes berserk – 'If only your father were here!' – and a weeping Cathy rushes to separate them, showing the habitual, demasculinising forces at work in the Brenner home that too rarely surface in the script. Before sealing themselves in for the night, Mitch and Melanie go out for firewood and pause on the porch to watch a giant formation of gulls flying overhead and heading inland, presumably toward sitting-duck Santa Rosa (whose dopey police classified Dan Fawcett's death as 'felony murder' during burglary). As they leave the house, in fact, the President can be heard obliviously speaking of other matters on the radio from Washington, suggesting the ineffectualness of political power when dealing with angry nature.

Attack night begins with Lydia stationed, like a priestess at the shrine, in a chair next to the piano beneath her husband's photograph. Annie's schoolroom was also overseen by a dead father figure, George Washington, the 'Father of His Country'. With Lydia so withdrawn, Cathy is sheltering with Melanie on the sofa, while faithful dog Mitch patrols the interior perimeter, latching, checking and reinforcing. (He has even, as we shall see, cleverly blocked the glass doors with huge barn doors.) It's a night watch or rather a wake. The lovebirds, with what Mrs Bundy called their 'small brain pans', have been exiled by a hostile Lydia to the kitchen with the rest of the pots. Resting next to the stove where so many of their brethren have been cooked, they peer amiably at the anxious Mitch as he passes by and seem as

comically delightful as Hitchcock's brace of dogs in the first scene. In a rare Hitchcock continuity error, the birds in close-up are decorously perched, while their cavorting, clambering shadow was just glimpsed against the kitchen door.

Dumbly reorienting herself by familiar domestic ritual, Lydia slowly gathers the cups and coffee pot onto a tray and carries it into the kitchen, flinching for a moment at the off-camera lovebirds inside the door. After she returns, Cathy starts to vomit (Lydia's cooking?), but her apathetic mother doesn't stir to help. It's Melanie who rushes Cathy off to the toilet and, when they return, is pressing a white napkin to the girl's forehead, just as Mitch stanched Melanie's bleeding in the restaurant. (Is it relevant that, as Spoto reports, 'from his childhood Hitchcock had a terror of vomiting'?)[96] Photographed at a tense angle, Lydia watches this transaction with chilly fatigue.

There is an arresting, low-angle wide-shot of Melanie's slender ankles and legs as she elegantly crosses them, with a lovely flex of the foot, while settling herself again on the sofa. Hitchcock cunningly accentuates the line of her legs with the barn door's wide, diagonal plank. It's a zoological tableau of legs: muscular Mitch on the piano bench hunches over his widespread thighs with animal readiness; Lydia, in fading, autumnal browns and greys, sits with legs stuck stiffly out like bowling pins, her knees curtained by a tweedy skirt; Cathy's prepubescent stick calves are clad in chaste, woolly, sky-blue kneesocks. Melanie, however, with her short, revealing skirt and stylish high heels, gracefully extends her long, smooth legs with their gleaming hose (soon to be pillaged), like the polished artifacts they are. We contemplate, as at the Eleusinian mysteries, the three stages of womanhood, from virginity through sexual maturity to sexual senescence.

Crisscross (the theme of *Strangers on a Train*): literally from the moment Melanie crosses her legs, the bird attack begins.[97] Has Lydia's witchy malice evoked it? Either a warning or a welcoming cheep comes from the unseen spectator lovebirds, as a deafening shrieking starts, reverberating like shaken sheet metal. When Lydia shakily stands up, Cathy instantly abandons Melanie, who seems to have lost her nerve, and throws herself into her mother's arms. Mother and daughter, rebonded, run frantically around the room like hunted animals (Hitchcock compared them to 'rats scurrying into corners'), eventually sinking down near the built-in shelves of books, which have no answers.[98] Lydia 'panics,' Hitchcock told Bogdanovich, because 'she is not strong, it is a facade': so architecturally, she is crumbling.[99]

Lacking the electronic soundtrack, Hitchcock had a musician do thunderous rolls on a miked side drum for the actors in this scene to have something to react to. Starting to lose her wits, Melanie shrinks back on the couch, drawing her legs up and finally rearing back to crush the lamp shade as she nearly swoons. Hitchcock said he chose the angles here 'to express the fear of the unknown', and he kept the camera back 'to show the nothingness from which she is shrinking'.[100] Melanie's movements are so floridly overwrought that she seems like the generic gal-turned-to-jelly of 50s screamer flicks, where women were always being delectably stalked by juvenile delinquents or space aliens. (Hitchcock makes Hedren repeat these gestures in *Marnie*, as she cowers on the sofa of the shipboard honeymoon suite.) Melanie ends up plastered to the mantelpiece like Lydia gone batty in the chimney attack. It's as if the house itself were aggressively haunted, as in a classic horror movie like *The Haunting* (1963).

Mitch, meanwhile, is a masculine whirlwind, getting his arms and hands bitten and gashed by birds, ripping out a lamp cord to bind the shutter, and nearly getting clawed by his own desperate, literally grasping, clutching mother as he firmly props her in an armchair (cf. Mrs Bates in her rocker). A convenient, hulking umbrella rack, mirrored like the diner cigarette machine, becomes his Dadaesque barrier against the Plywood Modern front door, which is being neatly drilled by gull beaks (actually awls manned by grips), with a shower of sawdust. Raymond Durgnat astutely compares the besieged Brenner house to the 'log-cabin' of America's fabled past, which is invaded here by the terrible 'beak-tomahawks' of bloodthirsty Indians.[101] Do the birds plan to turn the taxidermic tables? Hitchcock said that *Psycho*'s Norman 'filled his own mother with sawdust'.[102]

When the power suddenly goes off, apparently because the outside wires have been gnawed, the situation becomes grim. But the birds capriciously withdraw. 'They're going,' says Mitch with wonder, and we see one of the film's most stylised sequences: the heads of the three principals, side-lit in flickering chiaroscuro from the fireplace, are dramatically photographed from below. First, Mitch's face swings out of silhouette across a blank ceiling panel, which weighs down like the lid of a box or cage. Then Melanie's head, with shadows hollowing her cheekbones and contouring her shapely chin, hovers wide-eyed like Carl Dreyer's suffering Joan of Arc. When Lydia's head looms up into empty space, the camera pulls back to take in the three figures at full length, as they stand stock-still, listening, turned to stone like entombed colossi. They are as isolated as Giacometti spectres or Kon Tiki sentinels and as unified in shared fear as the survivors of the Blitz. The scene is as beautifully blocked as in live theatre.

All sense of time has been lost in the subterranean gloom. Nearly everyone is asleep, as the fire burns merrily in the hearth, the sole light and heat left to the cave-dwellers. Suddenly, the logs ominously break and collapse. Lydia is sleeping bolt upright on the piano stool, her head fallen forward corpse-like on her chest, looking just like the fierce Red Queen leaning heavily asleep and snoring on Alice. Cathy is curled up under a blanket on the sofa, and Mitch, looking like one of the damned from Michelangelo's 'Last Judgment', is slumped exhausted in a chair, his right hand on his groin and his head resting on his bandaged left hand – now sporting the heraldic white table napkin that has made the rounds from bird cage to infant brow. Only Melanie is awake, and once again she is the canary in the coal mine: hearing a flutter, she starts to call Mitch but decides to spare him. Picking up the torch that Mitch unearthed in the kitchen when the power failed (cf. Hitchcock's reference to Annie as 'the school teacher who's carrying a torch for him'), she checks the lovebirds first.[103] But when they prove quiet, she goes to the attic stairs to investigate. She moves as if hypnotically drawn to her quest. Some critics find Melanie's ascent foolhardy and self-destructive, but it seems to me a positive return to her early independence and initiative, when she had a flair for this kind of detective work. She is living up to her name – a Daniels who enters the lions' den.

As she hesitates before yet another unknocked door, Melanie's hand with its glossy crimson nails hovers near the knob, lit by torchlight. In her misty close-ups, Hedren again does the kind of magnetic, visibly apprehensive thinking that distinguished her performance at the jungle gym. As Hitchcock said of her performance in this film: 'There is not one redundant expression on Hedren's face. Every expression makes a point.'[104] The first thing Melanie sees when she opens the attic door is a ragged hole in the roof, through which shines the radiant blue sky. So it's dawn. A glimpse of light would normally mean deliverance in a science-fiction film such as *Journey to the Center of the Earth* (1959), but here it's

82 A gull giving Melanie a sadistic kiss in the attic

like a blasted bomb hole or a breakdown in a spaceship's radiation shields, through which evil forces rush from beyond. The blue square reminds me of the smashed brothel window in Picasso's 'Les Demoiselles d'Avignon', which also overlooks a sitting room of carnivorous creatures. The parallel within the film is the smashed window that Lydia first sees in Dan Fawcett's ransacked bedroom. When Melanie's torchlight scans the room, a horde of birds rises from the bed and rafters, and all hell breaks loose. It's the jungle gym again, but this time Melanie is trapped with the birds in the phone booth. The white canopy bed and children's book on the floor indicate that this is a young virgin's room, which has itself been gang-raped even before the mass assault begins on Melanie. As a sexual principle, bedrooms in *The Birds* are primal scenes of savagery.

The gulls and crows come storming at Melanie like a great wind, in undulations of sound. Hitchcock called for 'a menacing wave of vibration'.[105] We hear only the percussive flapping of wings, with very few bird cries and no scream whatever from Melanie. Sometimes the camera takes her view, so that birds with surreally gaping, almost unhinged jaws, fly directly in our face. Melanie tries to defend herself with the torch (symbolising her attempts to comprehend logically), which looks like the torch of the Statue of Liberty in *Saboteur* or the endangered light of freedom in Picasso's war-torn, animal-filled 'Guernica'. As her arm goes back and forth like a pendulum, the jumping beam creates a flashing, strobe-like effect in the chaotic room. It's like the failing windshield wipers and oncoming, blinking headlights of Marion's drive in *Psycho*. It also looks forward to the special effects in psychedelic discos, where sensory overload was a *sine qua non*: Melanie at times seems like one very strung-out partygoer, passing out as the other revellers rage on. And she prefigures another San Francisco newspaper heiress, Patty Hearst, who would be kidnapped and locked in a closet by her own pack of predators (the Symbionese Liberation Army) in 1974.

Arms raised (like the Christ images of *I Confess*), Melanie seems scourged and crucified simultaneously, her clothing shredded and her silky skin ripped by beaks. As it's punctured and pulled, her hosiery looks like a second skin being flayed. Calling out to Mitch too weakly to be heard (her last thought is for Cathy's safety), Melanie is slammed against the half-open door, which does wake the others. But as she sinks to the floor, in a wonderfully

choreographed cross-legged drop that completes the sequence from her sofa leg-cross, she blocks the door with her body, impeding her rescue. It's as if the room is underwater, and she is a swimmer swarmed by piranha or baby sharks. Wood sees 'voluptuous surrender and prostration' in her gestures, 'a despairing desire for annihilation'.[106]

By the time Mitch drags her out like a sack of potatoes (cf. *Frenzy*) or like Marion plastic-wrapped in *Psycho*, Melanie is being ravaged by birds jabbing at her breasts and furiously chewing on her lacquered fingertips. Comically disappearing last from view are her high heels: it's the last dance for the wily witch of the West. 'Oh, poor thing!' says Lydia (a phrase applied to birds by Annie and Mrs Bundy), who has courageously stood in the doorway batting back birds. Lying on the sofa downstairs, Melanie seems to have suffered a psychotic break. Eyes wide, she sees us and flails wildly at the camera, which jumps back to give her space: Hitchcock and we are yet more hungry birds. She's hallucinating, like a hippie chick on a bad trip. Like Annie, Mitch gives her brandy now, not peroxide, a bottle of which appears anyway in Lydia's hands as she sponges Melanie's wounds and binds her brow with bandages – the Oedipal wrap of blindman's buff. The socialite turned hobo has melted completely into birthday-girl Cathy.

Melanie's injuries, requiring medical aid, become a reason to flee Bodega Bay. Mitch steals out of the house with excruciating care past the burbling masses of birds lining fences, roofs and tree limbs. It's like a lynch mob forming outside the palace. Different species are indeed flocking together, as Mrs Bundy warned they never do. For this scene, Hitchcock said he wanted 'an electronic silence, a sort of monotonous low hum' to suggest the distant sea as well as 'the language of the birds'.[107] Like all the film's electronic effects, it was produced by the

Trautonium, an atonal keyboard designed by Remi Gassmann and Oskar Sala, with whom Hitchcock consulted for a month in West Berlin. Mitch fetches Melanie's car from the garage, which is oddly furnished with a skylight (a feature the birds-as-architects-unlicensed imposed on the bedroom). Lydia's metal-enclosed truck is not 'fast' enough (like its aging owner). Where's Mitch's hard-top car? – which would be a lot safer. Either it's at the diner, where it may have been incinerated in the parking lot, or at the Fawcett farm, from which Mitch may have got a quick police-car lift to the diner when Melanie called with news of the schoolhouse attack. In a Hitchcock film, such minor plot details are always deftly worked out.

On the car radio, Mitch hears that Bodega Bay is the epicentre of the disaster, that most people have gotten out, and that 'the military' may have to go in. There have been other attacks on Santa Rosa and Sebastopol: The 'attacks come in waves,' says the announcer, evoking images of civilisation sinking backward into the primal ocean. Some critics complain the sports car makes no noise as it emerges from the garage and pushes past the chattering birds: I do hear Mitch start the engine and give the accelerator a single burst, which gets the car moving but allows it to coast in neutral into the driveway.

Sitting mournfully in her fur coat like a moppet doll of Little Orphan Annie, her head wrapped in bandages like the newest look in scarf-tied turbans (with the chin strap of a dowager's overnight double-chin reducer), the catatonic Melanie often evokes laughter from an audience – which mortified scriptwriter Hunter when he first heard it. But this is Hitchcock's characteristic black humour, extorting from the audience an admission of our guilty pleasure in seeing the mighty fallen. Not even recognising her own car, which gleams in the pearly light like a fleet chariot of the sun god, Melanie panics at first sight of the bird yard and must be half-carried out, where she sinks into the tender arms of an apparently all-forgiving Lydia in the jumpseat. The scene recalls the end of *Notorious*, where the half-conscious heroine is also rescued from captivity in an upstairs bedroom and helped to a car under the suspicious gaze of Nazis in tuxedos – here a row of crows on a porch rail! Cathy's desire to bring the lovebirds along ('They haven't harmed anyone') is generally interpreted as a sign of hope for humanity's recovery, endorsed by early morning's rainbow beams. *The Birds* ends like *Psycho* with a shot of a car being extricated from Mother Nature's black morass.

So will the hostile audience of watchful birds turn doves of peace? But as the car roars away, their cries start up and rise to a sustained screech.

The psychological dynamics of the finale can be read in two ways. 'Lydia has become the mother Melanie never had', Wood says, but he asks whether Lydia's 'cradling' is 'a gesture of acceptance ... or a new maternal possessiveness' and whether the moment marks Melanie's 'development into true womanhood, or a final relapse into infantile dependence'.[108] Hedren declared to me about Lydia, 'I thought she accepted the daughter, and they lived happily ever after!' And Hedren firmly believed that Melanie would rebound: 'Melanie Daniels is a *strong woman* – absolutely!'

But I think Hitchcock has left the ending ambiguous: the two women's intimately intertwined hand and wrist (we see, from Lydia's point of view, Melanie's once-perfect nails now chipped like the titles) remind me of Mother's overlapping, wrist-clasping bronzed hands in the bedroom of *Psycho*, which ends with Mother in charge and her son in the loony bin. At the end of *The Birds*, who wields the claw? I agree with Margaret M. Horwitz's view that Lydia certainly appears 'victorious' and that she and the birds have 'achieved dominance'.[109] Melanie is now damaged goods, which Madonna Lydia prefers for her *pietà*. It's like the Pompeiian wall panels of the Villa of the Mysteries, where the exhausted, flagellated acolyte buries her face in the receptive maternal lap: rogue vixen Melanie has been whipped back to her biological place in the pecking order. Horwitz sees Melanie's eclipse in the film's treatment of her car: first, it gives her the 'power to come to Bodega Bay', then Mitch 'ends up driving it', and finally she's 'banished to the back seat' – becoming one of two children to Lydia as mother and Mitch as father (and Oedipal son). Oddly, when Mitch slips into the driver's seat, it's he who now seems the intruder, as his spidery hand startles Lydia from her dreamy communing with Melanie.

Hitchcock wanted the film to be literally open-ended, without 'THE END' indicated on screen, so as to leave the audience wondering. But the studio found this too confusing to preview audiences and ordered the rubric added. The current MCA Universal video has honoured Hitchcock's wishes by dropping it. If viewers are puzzled about what happens next in the story, it's no surprise, since the original script went on for at least ten more pages. A still-resentful Evan Hunter revealed that as the characters drove away, they passed through Bodega

Bay in 'absolute chaos', with victims in 'open shopdoors'; 'an overturned school bus'; a dead policeman draped over a roadblock; and a male corpse covered with birds on the beach. Attacked by birds, the car sped along the winding roads by which Melanie arrived. Catching up because they travel 'as the crow flies', the birds tore through the convertible roof, with the women, 'huddled inside crying', seen from above. When the road straightened out, the sports car could go faster than the birds and so escaped. The script ended optimistically, with the passengers spotting the clear, dawn sky in the distance.[110]

Hedren described to me how Hitchcock presented this finale, ultimately never shot, to the cast at the Santa Rosa Motel (an hour's drive from Bodega Bay), where the whole crew stayed and where her make-up and hair were done: 'I remember very, very well the evening he brought everybody into a meeting, and he talked about another ending. And it went on and on and on and *on*! And everyone said, "Oh, my God, this is never going to end!" He told us what we would see as we drove on.' She also recalls the Golden Gate Bridge being mentioned, although this detail is missing from Hunter's original script.

Are the bird attacks on Bodega Bay a freak phenomenon or a harbinger of global destruction? What relationship, if any, do they have to the ferocious psychodrama of female power? I see *The Birds* coming out of another film that was an embarrassing critical failure but that has had enormous influence on my thinking: Joseph Mankiewicz's *Suddenly, Last Summer* (1959), whose script, co-written by Gore Vidal, is based on an obscure Tennessee Williams play. It contains a jealous, possessive mother, Violet Venable (Katharine Hepburn), an imperious New Orleans aristocrat whose quasi-incestuous son-lover, the gay aesthete Sebastian, 'saw the face of God' – the annual slaughter of newly hatched sea turtles by 'a sky filled with savage, devouring birds' in the Galapagos Islands. 'Nature is cruel,' says Violet, remembering 'the noise of the birds, their horrible, savage cries as they circled': 'The killers inherited the earth.'

The lobotomy that Violet Venable tries to inflict on her niece, Catherine (Elizabeth Taylor), who saw Sebastian hacked to pieces and eaten by a wolf pack of boys, is in effect performed on Hitchcock's heroine in *The Birds*, who's out of her mind by the end. Violet's recognition of 'the horror of the truth' could serve as an epigraph for *The Birds*: 'We're all of us trapped by this devouring creation.'[111] A Williams line, spoken by Vivien Leigh in *The Roman Spring of Mrs Stone* (1961), also helps explain or justify Melanie Daniels' behaviour at her height: 'Beautiful people make their own laws.' It's a Wildean idea that perhaps only gay men and female Hellenophiles can understand.

Critics who think *The Birds* has no final meaning seem to be contradicted by Hitchock himself, whose comments about the film focus on its nature parable. Talking to Truffaut, he ascribed the real-life bird incidents to 'a form of rabies'.[112] He told another interviewer: 'All you can say about *The Birds* is nature can be awful rough on you. If you play around with it. Look what uranium has done. Men dug that out of the ground. *The Birds* expresses nature and what it can do, and the dangers of nature.'[113] And in a filmed interview, Hitchcock said:

> Basically, in *The Birds*, what you have is a kind of an overall sketchy theme of everyone taking nature for granted. Everyone took the birds for granted until the birds one day *turned* on them. The birds had been shot at, eaten, put in cages. They'd suffered *everything* from the humans, and it was time they turned *on* them. Don't mess about or tamper with nature. ...Who knows? It's feasible in the year 3000 or 4000 for *all* the animals to have taken over![114]

Hitchcock played on these ironies in the film's publicity campaign, which he masterminded. His voice intoned in a radio advertisement: 'If you have ever eaten a turkey drumstick, caged a canary or gone duck hunting, *The Birds* will give you something to think about.'[115] He also wrote the comically threatening ad line, which flummoxed studio flacks: '*The Birds* is coming!' This rebelliously fractured grammar seems perfect for a film in which a schoolteacher is assassinated. For the theatre lobby of the London premiere, he wanted a recording of that line played alongside two live, black mynah birds labelled Alfie and Tippi. In a print ad, Hitchcock tried sexual innuendo: 'There is a terrifying menace lurking right underneath the surface shock and suspense of *The Birds*. When you discover it, your pleasure will be more than doubled.'[116] It's the familiar Shakespearean paradox of shadow versus substance, but for Hitchcock, I suspect, the menace is archetypal woman, who is also mistress of surfaces.

On the official film poster, a huge, cruciform crow's shadow falls over the forehead of the screaming Lydia-turned-Melanie, who is being buzzed by a flock from the air. It is as if she were besieged by dark thoughts. As Marion Crane drives toward the motel in *Psycho*, she hears internalised voices – the superego of surprised lover, nosy cop and angry boss – just as Norman is maddened by the hectoring voice of his dead mother. *The Birds* is a quarrel between lovebirds and what Truffaut calls 'hate-filled birds', a battle among multiple, contradictory impulses.[117] Sometimes the birds in the film's process shots seem like black check marks, society's rules but also execution orders from the censoring pen of schoolmarm Mother Nature. Hitchcock said his method of cutting in advance in his head was 'just like a composer writes those little black dots' to make music.[118] Checks, dots, flecks, cuts: both the scissors that Grace Kelly uses to kill in *Dial M for Murder* and the straight razor (*à la Chien andalou*) with which Gregory Peck approaches sleeping Ingrid Bergman in *Spellbound* seem like open bird beaks. I think the peculiar quotation marks Hitchcock imposed on Hedren's first name (Tippi – a childhood nickname for her given name, Nathalie – became 'Tippi') look like diving birds, clef signs, and slashes of contraction. They are the director's lordly cuts and the acquisitive forceps by which he brought his star to birth.

Tippi Hedren's association with Hitchcock on his next project, *Marnie*, ended unpleasantly.[119] While she went on to make several more films with other directors, such as *The Harrad Experiment* (1973), her work for Hitchcock will stand as her creative peak. A strange story has entered popular lore of Hitchcock terrifying Hedren's small daughter, Melanie, with a miniature coffin containing a doll of her mother.[120] Hedren told me that the incident occurred at a private restaurant luncheon and that her daughter 'freaked out' and was 'very, very frightened by it'. However, the doll was not in a coffin but 'a very beautiful' pine box. Melanie reacted simply because 'it looked so real': the doll was an 'exact replica' of her mother, eyes open, dressed in the green suit from *The Birds*. Wax facial casts had previously been taken of Hedren in the studio make-up room without her knowing why. She maintains that the delicately crafted gift wasn't one of the director's notorious pranks but a sincere gesture that went badly: 'It wasn't a very happy experience,' she says, and Hitchcock was 'very upset'.

What of the striking fact that her character in *The Birds* is named Melanie? 'It has nothing to do with my daughter,' Hedren insisted to me. 'It was already in the script.' Scriptwriter Hunter himself calls it 'an odd

Publicity shot of Alfred Hitchcock and Tippi Hedren

coincidence'.[121] But the script was apparently not finalised until early 1962, months after Hedren's screen test.[122] Collapsing the generations into one identity is a mind game that, as we have seen, Hitchcock liked to play. Indeed, the name of Hedren's next role strangely collapsed the heroines' names from the two prior films. Marion, Melanie, Marnie: is this an unholy Trinity, with Melanie crucified between two thieves? If we read Marion as 'Mary', there are also biblical echoes in the lead names of the two films preceding *Psycho*: Madeleine (Magdalene) in *Vertigo* and Eve in *North by Northwest*. Constance Porter, Melanie Daniels' fur-clad precursor in *Lifeboat*, is also twinned with Constance Peterson, the heroine of Hitchcock's next film, *Spellbound*. Constancy is precisely what Hitchcock the artist did *not* see in women.

Curiously, Hedren and her then-husband, agent Noel Marshall, later founded an animal preserve in Soledad Canyon in Acton, California, forty miles north of Los Angeles. Though it began as a movie set, Shambala became a refuge for nearly 100 wild animals, mainly lions and tigers, whose care and adventures she chronicled in her lavishly illustrated 1985 book, *The Cats of Shambala*. Hedren describes going to meetings, interviews, supermarkets, and even a 'posh restaurant' with a baby lion in a picnic basket; being clawed in the face and scarred by a cheetah; having her scalp gashed open by a lion seizing her head in its jaws; and developing gangrene after her leg was crushed by an elephant. There are photos of Hedren and the adolescent Melanie playing rowdy tug-of-war with four lion cubs in the bedroom, and of Melanie sleeping with a giant, full-grown lion under a blanket in bed, its heavy tail curving to the floor. 'Lions, Lions, and More Lions' is one chapter title in the book.[123]

Talking to Truffaut, Hitchcock dismissed the plot contrivances of his own films as an arbitrary 'MacGuffin'. He told the story of a man on a train claiming a package in the baggage rack to be a MacGuffin, 'an apparatus for trapping lions in the Scottish Highlands'. Another man says, 'But there are no lions in the Scottish Highlands'. The first one replies, 'Well, then, that's no MacGuffin!' Thus a MacGuffin, said Hitchcock, was 'actually nothing at all'.[124]

In many interviews over the years about *Psycho*, Janet Leigh has repeatedly expressed her continuing fear of taking showers. Tippi Hedren, in contrast, although traumatised by animal nature in *The Birds*, seems to have actively confronted Hitchcock's challenges. Once her

Hedren triumphant

'consciousness had been raised' about animals, she wrote, she refused to wear the fur coat Hitchcock had given her and eventually 'hocked' it to pay feed and maintenance bills at Shambala. As queen of the lions, she beat Hitchcock at his own game: of all his stars, she is the only one who found the MacGuffin. And in her embattled private dialogue with Hitchcock, Tippi Hedren has had the last word.

APPENDIX

. . . .

Melanie Daniels' Social Calendar

FRIDAY   *3.0 p.m.*: Davidson's Pet Shop, San Francisco. Melanie
arrives to pick up mynah bird. Meets Mitchell Brenner.
Lets canary escape in shop. Orders lovebirds for delivery
next morning.

SATURDAY   *Early morning*: Melanie takes lovebirds to Mitch's
apartment building and learns he's gone home for
weekend. She makes two-hour drive to Bodega Bay by
coast road.
Late morning: Brinkmayer's General Store, Bodega Bay.
First visit to Annie Hayworth's. Melanie crosses bay by
rented boat. Leaves lovebirds at Brenner house.
Lunchtime: Melanie pursued by Mitch in car around bay.
She is hit by gull in boat. While being treated in restaurant,
she meets Lydia Brenner and is invited to dinner by Mitch.
After lunch: Annie's again. Melanie asks to rent room for
one night.
7.0 p.m.: Melanie has dinner at the Brenners.
Late night: Melanie back at Annie's for the night. Gull hits
front door.

SUNDAY   *Afternoon*: Cathy's birthday party on the Brenner lawn.
Birds attack the children.
Dinnertime: Brenners and Melanie with sandwiches. Birds
fly down chimney and erupt from fireplace.
Overnight: Melanie stays at the Brenners.

MONDAY   *Early morning*: Lydia drops Cathy at school and visits Dan
Fawcett's farmhouse. Finds him dead from overnight bird
attack.
Mid-morning: Melanie serves tea to Lydia prostrated in
bed.
Late morning: Melanie goes to pick up Cathy at
schoolhouse. Sees crows massing on jungle gym. Crow
attack on children running in road.

Lunchtime: Melanie calls her father from restaurant. Gull hits mechanic pumping gas, leading to explosion and fire. Melanie trapped in telephone booth as gulls attack. Melanie ostracised by women in restaurant. Annie found dead at her house.
Late afternoon: Mitch boards up the Brenner house as Melanie helps.
Late evening: Massive bird attack on the Brenner house. Front door and windows nearly broken through.

TUESDAY
Dawn: Bird attack on Melanie in the Brenner attic, rendering her catatonic.
Early morning: Brenners and the wounded Melanie flee in her car.

NOTES

· ·

1 Quoted in Donald Spoto, *The Art of Alfred Hitchcock* (New York: Doubleday, 1992), p. 330.
2 Of costume dramas like his *Waltzes from Vienna* (1933), Hitchcock said, 'I hate this kind of film, and I have no feeling for it'. Quoted in Eric Rohmer and Claude Chabrol, *Hitchcock: The First Forty-Four Films*, trans. Stanley Hochman (1957; New York: F. Ungar, 1979), p. 37.
3 Daphne du Maurier, 'The Birds', in *Kiss Me Again, Stranger* (New York: Doubleday, 1952), p. 32.
4 François Truffaut, *Hitchcock* (New York: Simon and Schuster, 1967), p. 217. In screenwriter Evan Hunter's original plan, a newly arrived schoolteacher is the focus of the bird attacks. 'But Hitch did not want a schoolteacher for his lead; he needed someone more sophisticated and glamorous.' Evan Hunter, *Me and Hitch* (London: Faber and Faber, 1997), p. 14.
5 Du Maurier, 'The Birds', pp. 40, 43.
6 Peter Bogdanovich, *The Cinema of Alfred Hitchcock* (New York: Museum of Modern Art Film Library, 1963), p. 44.
7 'On Style: An Interview with *Cinema*', from *Cinema* vol. 1, no. 5, Aug–Sept 1963, in *Hitchcock on Hitchcock: Selected Writings and Interviews*, ed. Sidney Gottlieb (Berkeley: University of California Press, 1995), p. 295.
8 Du Maurier, 'The Birds', pp. 35–6.
9 Bogdanovich, *The Cinema of Alfred Hitchcock*, p. 44.
10 Du Maurier, 'The Birds', pp. 52, 36, 66.
11 In another kind of performance in *Murder!* (1930), the caped trapeze artist who emerges wearing a huge headdress of ostrich feathers turns out to be a man.
12 Donald Spoto, *The Dark Side of Genius: The Life of Alfred Hitchcock* (Boston: Little, Brown, 1983), pp. 371, 31. Evan Hunter says Hitchcock's wife, Alma Reville, 'fluttered about like a bird herself'. Hunter, *Me and Hitch*, p. 38.
13 Spoto, *The Dark Side of Genius*, p. 444. My inquiries to libraries and newspaper offices in the Santa Cruz and La Jolla areas could not confirm the date (27 April 1960) given by Spoto, p. 563n.

14 Philip K. Scheuer, 'Hitchcock's "Birds" Begin War on Man', *Los Angeles Times*, March 22, 1962; 'Falcon Scares Children', *Los Angeles Herald-Examiner*, 22 March, 1962.
15 Truffaut, *Hitchcock*, p. 17.
16 Spoto, *The Dark Side of Genius*, pp. 40, 192n.
17 Truffaut, *Hitchcock*, pp. 192–3.
18 'On Style', in *Hitchcock on Hitchcock*, p. 300.
19 Janet Leigh with Christopher Nickens, *Psycho: Behind the Scenes of the Classic Thriller* (New York: Harmony Books, 1995), p. 26.
20 Ibid., p. 42.
21 Truffaut, *Hitchcock*, p. 239. Art director Robert Boyle said: 'Hitchcock is always trying to make the visual statement. Each shot must make its statement, it must relate to all the other shots, and there is no such thing as a throwaway shot. That was the major truth I learned from working with Hitchcock.' Quoted in Mary Corliss and Carlos Clarens, 'Designed for Film: The Hollywood Art Director', *Film Comment* vol. 14, no. 4, May/June 1978, p. 33.
22 Spoto, *The Dark Side of Genius*, p. 451.
23 'The Making of *The Birds*', *Cinefantastique* vol. 10, no. 2, Fall 1980, pp. 22–3. This is the best source for technical information about *The Birds*.
24 Ibid., p. 23; Spoto, *The Dark Side of Genius*, p. 348.
25 Spoto, ibid., p. 405.
26 Truffaut, *Hitchcock*, p. 197. Evan Hunter, carrying his typewriter and 'the almost finished script of *The Birds*', also had to flee his rented Brentwood home with his wife. The fire 'threatened to leap Sunset Boulevard to create a true holocaust'. Hunter, *Me and Hitch*, pp. 44–6.
27 Bogdanovich, *The Cinema of Alfred Hitchcock*, p. 45.
28 Robert Boyle, quoted in Corliss, 'Designed for Film', p. 35.
29 'It's a Bird. It's a Plane. It's …"The Birds"', in *Hitchcock on Hitchcock*, p. 317.
30 Spoto, *The Dark Side of Genius*, p. 459.
31 Counts, 'The Making of *The Birds*', p. 33.

32 Spoto, *The Dark Side of Genius*, p. 458.

33 Telephone interview, 15 October 1997. Hedren at Shambala, Acton, CA; Camille Paglia in Philadelphia. All other references to my conversation with Hedren are from this interview.

34 *Films Illustrated* vol. 1, no. 3, September 1971, p. 22. Quoted in Spoto, *The Dark Side of Genius*, p. 464.

35 Counts, 'The Making of *The Birds*', p. 33.

36 Ibid.

37 Ibid., pp. 20–1.

38 Ibid., p. 21.

39 Spoto, *The Dark Side of Genius*, p. 455. Five of Boyle's watercolour and charcoal sketches are reproduced in Counts, 'The Making of *The Birds*', p. 19. They show du Maurier's Hocken crossing a wooden seaside bridge with his daughter, pursued by gulls and spied on by crows lurking in the reeds.

40 Counts, ibid., p. 17.

41 'It's a Bird', p. 317. Whitlock's matte for the scene, along with others, is reproduced in colour in Counts, ibid., pp. 24–5.

42 The Universal Hotel, according to Boyle, was later built on that hill. Boyle describes how 'miniature smoke' had to be painstakingly photographed and timed to go through the matte and join with the real smoke: 'I think this was the most difficult shot with special photographic problems ever made. It was a fanciful shot, a fantastic shot, but a very real one. … All [Hitchcock's] films have that sense of verisimilitude. He bends reality to his purpose to get the real truth.' Quoted in Corliss, 'Designed for Film', pp. 34–5.

43 'On Style', in *Hitchcock on Hitchcock*, p. 300.

44 'It's a Bird', ibid., p. 315.

45 Spoto, *The Dark Side of Genius*, p. 454.

46 Counts, 'The Making of *The Birds*', p. 34.

47 Ibid., p. 17.

48 Bogdanovich, *The Cinema of Alfred Hitchcock*, p. 45.

49 Quoted in Counts, 'The Making of *The Birds*', p. 22.

50 Hitchcock captures another winged figure outlined against the veiled sky in *Sabotage*: the statue of Eros atop the Shaftesbury fountain in London's Piccadilly Circus, which is targeted for a terrorist bombing in the film. I am grateful to the San Francisco History Center of the San Francisco Public Library for help with information about the Dewey Monument. At the famous St Francis Hotel on the west side of Union Square, just north of Hitchcock's pet shop, silent-film comedy star Fatty Arbuckle threw a wild party in 1921 that led to the death of a young actress. *The Penguin Guide to San Francisco and Northern California*, ed. Alan Tucker (New York: Penguin Books, 1991), p. 32.

51 I am grateful to Elaine Burrows of the National Film and Television Archive in London for identifying the breed of Hitchcock's dogs, about which critical sources differ.

52 Truffaut, *Hitchcock*, p. 217.

53 Robin Wood, *Hitchcock's Films Revisited* (New York: Columbia University Press, 1989), p. 155. I am grateful to Prof. John DeWitt of the University of the Arts for identifying Melanie's sports car. Drawing on his formidable expertise in automobile history, DeWitt states: 'It is an Aston-Martin DB2/4 (the '4' refers to the fact that it could fit four people, although they had to be extremely small and thin). While I would need to examine the brakes and chrome strips, it is probably a Mark II, which was produced in 1955 and 1956. Only 24 MKII dropheads (convertibles) were produced. It cost $6250 brand new, a lot of money in 1955, when a Porsche 1500s speedster cost only $3500. It would be an older and exotic car which would say a lot about her (since she could expect it to break down about every 150 miles). It's a real aficionado's car, known for its handling, but it requires skill. It is not a car that suggests fashion, superficiality, or trendiness. It's definitely not a girly pseudo-sports car like a Thunderbird two-seater.' What of James Bond's Aston-Martin? ('Dr. No', the first film based on Ian Fleming's Bond novels, was released in 1962.) DeWitt notes that Bond's car was 'a DB4 and a fastback coupe, not a convertible'. Nonetheless, Melanie's Bond-like sports car certainly reinforces her character as a cosmopolitan sexual adventuress.

54 Elizabeth Weis, *The Silent Scream: Alfred Hitchcock's Sound Track* (East Brunswick, NJ: Fairleigh Dickinson University Press, 1982), pp. 17, 19, 142.

55 See 'Bodega Bay Area Map & Guide', published by the Bodega Bay Area Chamber of Commerce, 850 Coast Highway 1, Bodega Bay, CA 94923.

56 The preliminary storyboards gave Bodega Bay more contemporary automobiles than those that were used for the film. See illustrations in Counts, 'The Making of *The Birds*', p. 27.

57 Truffaut, *Hitchcock*, p. 205.

58 In *Sabotage*, a bomb is in fact delivered hidden in the bottom of a bird cage.

59 Evan Hunter confirms that his 'reference points' in writing the script were indeed 'the black and white comedies I'd grown up with in the forties: Cary Grant and Irene Dunne, Cary Grant and Katharine Hepburn, Cary Grant and Ginger Rogers'. Hunter, *Me and Hitch*, p. 19. However, Hunter's continuing refusal to acknowledge Tippi Hedren's contributions to *The Birds* is most regrettable.

60 Counts, 'The Making of *The Birds*', p. 28.

61 'On Style', in *Hitchcock on Hitchcock*, p. 300.

62 Bogdanovich, *The Cinema of Alfred Hitchcock*, pp. 43–4.

63 Truffaut, *Hitchcock*, p. 114.

64 Wood, *Hitchcock's Films Revisited*, p. 159.

65 Spoto, *The Dark Side of Genius*, p. 461.

66 In *Sabotage*, the little boy who receives the gift of two caged birds asks his father, "Which one's the hen? Wouldn't it be funny if the gent one day laid an egg?'

67 Spoto, *The Dark Side of Genius*, pp. 36–7, 464.

68 Ibid., p. 23.

69 Suzanne Pleshette had just finished filming *Rome Adventure* (released in 1962), in which she played a school librarian fired for giving a student a censored book.

70 Bogdanovich, *The Cinema of Alfred Hitchcock*, pp. 43–4.

71 Counts, 'The Making of *The Birds*', p. 18. Deeming the scene 'totally inept and devoid of

any craftsmanship', Hunter now says he thinks Hitchcock wrote it. However, he also blames actor Hume Cronyn and writer/critic V.S. Pritchett (whom Hitchcock privately consulted) for meddling in the script. Slighting Cronyn's wife, Jessica Tandy, Hunter oddly calls her fine portrayal of Lydia Brenner 'one of the few bad performances she ever gave in her life'. Hunter, *Me and Hitch*, pp. 70, 55–6, 60–1, 65, 30.

72 Spoto, *The Art of Alfred Hitchcock*, p. 334.

73 See Camille Paglia, *Sexual Personae: Art and Decadence from Nefertiti to Emily Dickinson* (New Haven: Yale University Press, 1990), p. 51.

74 Wood, *Hitchcock's Films Revisited* p. 165.

75 Truffaut, *Hitchcock*, p. 219.

76 Ibid., p. 220. While this scene was actually shot and edited out later, other scenes in Evan Hunter's first draft were rejected a priori by Hitchcock as 'undramatic'. I particularly mourn the loss of what Hunter describes as 'a scene between Melanie and her father in his newspaper office' (pp. 46–9).

77 'On Style', in *Hitchcock on Hitchcock*, p. 301; Truffaut, *Hitchcock*, pp. 111, 224.

78 Truffaut, *Hitchcock*, p. 216.

79 Bogdanovich, *The Cinema of Alfred Hitchcock*, p. 4.

80 'On Style', in *Hitchcock on Hitchcock*, p. 301.

81 Wood, *Hitchcock's Films Revisited*, p. 164.

82 Counts, 'The Making of *The Birds*', p. 28. Inside and on the back cover are startling photos of Hedren and Pleshette in their gruesome make-up.

83 Ibid., p. 28. Eighteen storyboards from this scene are reproduced.

84 Bogdanovich, *The Cinema of Alfred Hitchcock*, p. 44.

85 Hitchcock's architectural symbolism is evident as early as *Murder!* (1930), which ends with a magnificent shot of a stony prison facade. As a British Romantic, he inherited from William Blake and Charles Dickens that understanding of prison spaces traced by so many ill-informed persons to Michel Foucault.

86 Counts, 'The Making of *The Birds*', p. 30.

87 When the birds attack the birthday party, Mitch and Melanie ditch the two martini glasses against the sand bank. Is this a Surrealist pun by Hitchcock on his motif of fallen eyeglasses?

88 Truffaut, *Hitchcock*, p. 221. Hunter felt this wonderful piece of work was 'his best scene' in the film. He wrote it, at Hitchcock's request, two months after the first draft had been completed and submitted. Counts, 'The Making of *The Birds*', p. 18. Hunter, *Me and Hitch*, pp. 54–5.

89 Mrs Ward, a juror in *Murder!*, strikingly looks and speaks like a younger Mrs Bundy. The actresses playing the 'Jury Ladies' are grouped together in the credits: Violet Farebrother, Claire Greet and Drusilla Wills.

90 'Cage of misery' is Hitchcock's phrase in Truffaut, *Hitchcock*, p. 217. See *Blackmail*, with its tell-tale 'detectives in glass houses' – actually a phone booth inside a tobacco shop.

91 Ibid.

92 Ibid., p. 221.

93 Bogdanovich, *The Cinema of Alfred Hitchcock*, p. 44.

94 Truffaut, *Hitchcock*, p. 222.

95 The female proprietor of the bird shop in *Sabotage* says of another character, 'It's her cross, and she must bear it. We all have our cross to bear'.

96 Spoto, *The Dark Side of Genius*, p. 82.

97 The crisscrossing double-murder plot of *Strangers on a Train* is symbolised by the crossed tennis rackets heraldically embossed on a cigarette lighter. In *Un Chien andalou*, a tennis racket is hung like a crucifix on a wall, expressing the Surrealist insight that social institutions and philosophical systems are a game (another discovery wrongly attributed to poststructuralism).

98 Truffaut, *Hitchcock*, p. 218.

99 Bogdanovich, *The Cinema of Alfred Hitchcock*, p. 44.

100 'On Style', in *Hitchcock on Hitchcock*, p. 291; Truffaut, p. 200.

101 Raymond Durgnat, *The Strange Case of Alfred Hitchcock* (Cambridge, Mas.: M.I.T. Press, 1974), p. 340.

102 Truffaut, *Hitchcock*, p. 211.

103 Bogdanovich, *The Cinema of Alfred Hitchcock*, p. 43.

104 Ibid., p. 5.

105 Truffaut, *Hitchcock*, p. 224.

106 Wood, *Hitchcock's Films Revisited*, pp. 170–1.

107 Truffaut, *Hitchcock*, pp. 224–5.

108 Wood, *Hitchcock's Films Revisited*, p. 172.

109 Margaret M. Horwitz, '*The Birds*: A Mother's Love', in Marshall Deutelbaum and Leland Poague (eds), *A Hitchcock Reader* (Ames, Iowa: Iowa State University Press, 1986), p. 286. This fine essay is one of the best analyses of Hitchcock I have found during my research.

110 Counts, 'The Making of *The Birds*', pp. 34–5. Three of the script pages are shown. Reproducing his original ending, Hunter testily says V.S. Pritchett was responsible for the 'gloomier', truncated ending of the final film. Hunter, *Me and Hitch*, pp. 40, 64–6.

111 Sea turtles actually appear in *Sabotage*: their tank at the Aquarium of the London Zoo is the point of rendezvous for two evil conspirators plotting a bombing that will destroy a crowded city bus, killing the little boy of the film.

112 Truffaut, *Hitchcock*, p. 216.

113 'On Style', in *Hitchcock on Hitchcock*, p. 294.

114 *Inside Hitchcock* (1973), from *The Men Who Made the Movies*, series produced by The American Cinematheque, HPI Home Video.

115 Counts, 'The Making of *The Birds*', p. 33.

116 Ibid., p. 26.

117 Truffaut, *Hitchcock*, p. 218.

118 'Inside Hitchcock' (video).

119 See Spoto, *The Dark Side of Genius*, pp. 468–76.

120 The rumours probably began in 1983 with careless reviews of Donald Spoto's excellent biography of Hitchcock, *The Dark Side of Genius*. His synopsis of the doll incident (pp. 467–8) differs slightly from Tippi Hedren's account of it to me.

121 Hunter, *Me and Hitch*, p. 23.

122 Spoto, *The Dark Side of Genius*, pp. 452–3. Claiming he named the character

Melanie, while Hitchcock called her 'The Girl', Hunter as usual avoids any association with Tippi Hedren, whom he attaches to the initial chilly critical reception of *The Birds* and *Marnie*. Since barely three weeks elapsed between his reporting to work on *The Birds* and Hedren's first interview, and since Hitchcock himself conceived the Melanie character during that time, the issue remains cloudy. That Hunter's recollections are not always reliable is suggested by his saying of Daphne du Maurier's original story, 'There was not a line of dialogue in it' – when, in fact,

the story is packed with dialogue. Hunter, *Me and Hitch*, pp. 23, 12, 10.

123 Tippi Hedren with Theodore Taylor, *The Cats of Shambala: The Extraordinary Story of Life with the Big Cats* (New York: McGraw Hill, 1985), pp. 86, 97, 127, 196, 54, 41, 27, 146. I was stunned to learn about Hedren's Shambala from the TV show, *Lifestyles of the Rich and Famous* (December 1987). Lost, alas, in a disastrous 1978 flood at the preserve was the black-and-white TV commercial that first brought Hedren to Hitchcock's attention (p. 226).

124 Truffaut, *Hitchcock*, pp. 98–9.

Hitchcock and the electronic Trautonium used in *The Birds*

CREDITS

· ·

The Birds

USA
1963

Production Company
Alfred J. Hitchcock
Productions Inc
US Release
28 March 1963
US Distributor
Universal Pictures
UK Release
September 1963
UK Distributor
Rank /
Universal-International

Production Manager
Norman Deming
Director
Alfred Hitchcock
Assistant Director
James H. Brown
**Assistant to Mr
Hitchcock**
Peggy Robertson
Script Supervisor
Lois Thurman
Screenplay
Evan Hunter
Based on a story by Daphne
du Maurier
Director of Photography
Robert Burks
**Special Photographic
Adviser**
Ub Iwerks
Editor
George Tomasini
Special Effects
Lawrence A. Hampton
Production Designer
Robert Boyle
Set Decorator
George Milo
Pictorial Design
Albert Whitlock
Wardrobe Supervisor
Rita Riggs

**Miss Hedren's Costume
Designer**
Edith Head
Make-up
Howard Smit
Hairstylist
Virginia Darcy
Titles
James S. Pollak
**Electronic Sound
Production/Composition**
Remi Gassmann, Oskar Sala
Sound Consultant
Bernard Herrmann
Sound Recording
Waldon O. Watson, William
Russell
Bird Trainer
Ray Berwick

Rod Taylor
Mitch Brenner
Jessica Tandy
Lydia Brenner
Suzanne Pleshette
Annie Hayworth
'Tippi' Hedren
Melanie Daniels
Veronica Cartwright
Cathy Brenner
Ethel Griffies
Mrs Bundy
Charles McGraw
Sebastian Sholes
Ruth McDevitt
Mrs MacGruder
Lonny Chapman
Deke Carter
Joe Mantell
traveling salesman
Doodles Weaver
fisherman
Malcolm Atterbury
Deputy Al Malone
John McGovern
postal clerk
Karl Swenson
drunk in bar

Richard Deacon
Mitch's neighbour in elevator
Elizabeth Wilson
Helen Carter
William Quinn
farmhand
Doreen Lang
hysterical mother in restaurant
Morgan Brittany
schoolchild

[uncredited]
Alfred Hitchcock
man leaving pet shop
with two West Highland
White Terriers (Geoffrey
& Stanley)

In Colour
Technicolor

10,710 feet
119 minutes

Credits compiled by
Markku Salmi.

The print of *The Birds* in
the National Film and
Television Archive was
acquired specially for the
360 Classic Feature Films
project from studio
negatives through Universal
International Pictures.

BIBLIOGRAPHY

. . . .

Bogdanovich, Peter, *The Cinema of Alfred Hitchcock* (New York: The Museum of Modern Art Film Library, 1963).

Counts, Kyle B., 'The Making of *The Birds*' (additional material by Steve Rubin), *Cinefantastique* vol. 10, no. 2, Fall 1980.

du Maurier, Daphne, 'The Birds', in *Kiss Me Again, Stranger* (New York: Doubleday, 1952).

Durgnat, Raymond, *The Strange Case of Alfred Hitchcock* (Cambridge, Mass.: M.I.T. Press, 1974).

Gottlieb, Sidney (ed.), *Hitchcock on Hitchcock: Selected Writings and Interviews* (Berkeley: University of California Press, 1995).

Hedren, Tippi, with Theodore Taylor, *The Cats of Shambala: The Extraordinary Story of Life with the Big Cats* (New York: McGraw Hill, 1985).

Horwitz, Margaret M., ' *The Birds*: A Mother's Love', in Marshall Deutelbaum and Leland Poague (eds), *A Hitchcock Reader* (Ames, Iowa: Iowa State University Press, 1986).

Hunter, Evan, *Me and Hitch* (London: Faber and Faber, 1997).

Inside Hitchcock (1973), from *The Men Who Made the Movies*, series produced by The American Cinematheque, HPI Home Video.

Leigh, Janet, with Christopher Nickens, *Psycho: Behind the Scenes of the Classic Thriller* (New York: Harmony Books, 1995).

Los Angeles Herald-Examiner, 'Falcon Scares Children', March 22, 1962.

Paglia, Camille, *Sexual Personae: Art and Decadence from Nefertiti to Emily Dickinson* (New Haven: Yale University Press, 1990).

Rohmer, Eric and Claude Chabrol, *Hitchcock: The First Forty-four Films* (1957), trans. Stanley Hochman (New York: Frederick Ungar, 1979).

Santa Cruz Sentinel, 'Seabird Invasion Hits Coastal Homes', August 18, 1961.

Scheuer, Philip K., 'Hitchcock's "Birds" Begin War on Man', *Los Angeles Times*, March 22, 1962.

Spoto, Donald, *The Art of Alfred Hitchcock* (New York: Doubleday, 1992).

——————, *The Dark Side of Genius: The Life of Alfred Hitchcock* (Boston: Little, Brown, 1983).

Truffaut, François, in collaboration with Helen G. Scott, *Hitchcock* (New York: Simon Schuster, 1967).

Tucker, Alan (ed.), *The Penguin Guide to San Francisco and Northern California* (New York: Penguin Books, 1991).

Weis, Elizabeth, *The Silent Scream: Alfred Hitchcock's Sound Track* (East Brunswick, NJ: Fairleigh Dickinson University Press, 1982).

Wood, Robin, *Hitchcock's Films Revisited* (New York: Columbia University Press, 1989).

ALSO PUBLISHED

If you would like further information about future BFI Film Classics or about other books on film, media and popular culture from BFI Publishing, please write to:

BFI Film Classics
BFI Publishing
21 Stephen Street
London W1P 2LN

Each book in the BFI Publishing Film Classics series honours a great film from the history of world cinema. With new titles published each year, the series is rapidly building into a collection representing some of the best writing on film. If you would like to receive further information about future Film Classics or about other books on film, media and popular culture from BFI Publishing, please fill in your name and address and return this card to the BFI.* (No stamp required if posted in the UK, Channel Islands, or Isle of Man.)

NAME

ADDRESS

POSTCODE

E-MAIL ADDRESS:

WHICH *BFI FILM CLASSIC* DID YOU BUY?

* In North America and Asia (except India),
please return your card to:
University of California Press, Web Department,
2120 Berkeley Way, Berkeley, CA 94720, USA

BFI Publishing
21 Stephen Street
FREEPOST 7
LONDON
W1E 4AN